GET THE EDGE

Audrey Bakewell

GET THE EDGE

Audrey Bakewell's

POWER SKATING

TECHNIQUE

POLESTAR
BOOK PUBLISHERS

GET THE EDGE

Polestar Book Publishers acknowledges the support from the publishing
programs of the Canada Council, the British Columbia Ministry of Small
Business, Tourism and Culture, and the Department of Canadian Heritage.

Thanks also to everyone at the Burnaby Winter Club, Great Pacific Forum and
Eight Rinks for your cooperation in the photo sessions for this book.

Cover photographs by Chris Relke.
Interior photographs by Chris Relke, where indicated.
Cover design by Jim Brennan.
All illustrations and diagrams by Jim Brennan.
Printed in Canada by Best Book Manufacturers.

CANADIAN CATALOGUING IN PUBLICATION DATA
Bakewell, Audrey Elaine, 1954-
      Get the edge
ISBN 1-896095-21-6
      1. Skating I. Title.
GV849.B34 1996   796.91   C96-910413-8

POLESTAR BOOK PUBLISHERS
1011 Commercial Drive, Second Floor
Vancouver, British Columbia
Canada V5L 3X1
(604) 251-9718 / Fax (604) 251-9738

5 4 3 2 1

I dedicate this book to my mother, Irene Bakewell, who over the years answered calls, took messages, mailed brochures, helped count and bag jerseys, hauled equipment, pylons and pucks, and accompanied me to countless practices, clinics, games, and hockey functions.

Thank you for all of your help and encouragement.

GET THE EDGE

PREFACE

BRIAN J. GAVRILOFF

People always ask me, "How did you ever get involved in hockey?"

Well, at the time I was a figure skater and my knowledge of hockey consisted of the opinion that hockey players wrecked the ice and could not tell time. The old Edmonton Gardens was our favourite rink for extra ice time. Our sessions on the weekend were often before or after the Edmonton Oil King games. We used to come to the rink dressed, skates on, ready to go — often to find the hockey game still on.

We had no concept of overtime and used to lean over the boards and yell, "Hey, get off the ice, your ice time's finished." Then we would point to our watches and the big clock, get a little more verbal and definitely louder, "Hey, stupid, can't you tell time, get off the ice."

Needless to say we would catch the attention of several players, especially the visiting team who was not accustomed to our ranting. The player closest to the boards often made the mistake of looking over at us and then BOOM, one of the Oil Kings would get in an unexpected punch and the melee was on. It got to the point that as soon as we showed up in the rink the play would move to the corner where we entered and the home team would again take advantage of our routine.

Occasionally we were on the ice before the game, and fans would come early to watch us skate. Our coach took advantage of this opportunity to have us practice performing. Before professional hockey came to the Edmonton Gardens, the ice was very soft — a figure skater's dream because you could really dig into the ice and get great lift without taking a big chunk out of the ice. We used to skate our hearts out at the Gardens.

Our favourite hockey team was the Calgary Centennials because they convinced their coach to arrive early so that they could watch us perform. We, of course, thought it was because we were such good skaters. I realize now that it was probably due more to the fact that because the old Gardens was so warm we wore as little as possible.

My direct involvement with hockey be-

Audrey Bakewell and Japan's Seibu Bunnies, visiting Edmonton in 1991

gan in the early 1970s when my brother, Brian, asked on behalf of his hockey coach, Ken Weech, if I would come out and give his team some tips. At that point I realized that if my brother's team needed help, so did others. Next came some demonstrations at the Bruce MacGregor Hockey School. Bruce encouraged me to continue on with my interest in hockey.

During my last year of university I had space for an option and could fill it with a psychology or a hockey course. Encouragement from Golden Bear hockey coach Leon Abbott sealed my fate — I signed up for the hockey course. Halfway through the course, Coach Abbott asked if I was interested in teaching some classes. Thinking that he meant while he was on the road, I figured, Hey—no problem. I can cover a couple of classes for him. So my answer was "Sure." I remember him saying that I could only do it on the condition that I pull my weight the same as a man, and that I realize I will always have to be better than any man on the ice. As it turned out, Coach Abbott wanted me to work at the hockey school as a hockey instructor. So I turned professional to teach hockey and develop my own power skating program.

Each player in the class would pass along his hockey secret to me, so I was learning from more than Coach Abbott. Rather than admit how little I knew, I proceeded through the course imitating everyone in the class. For example, I noticed that often a player would stand close to the goalie in front of the net, tap his stick, yell for the puck, receive the pass and score.

I decided I wanted to score a goal, so when everyone else was at the other end I went over by the goalie to yell and wave for the puck. The goalie asked me what the hell I was doing. I told him that I was planning to score on him. The whistle went and Coach Abbott motioned me over.

"Don't you know what offside is?" he asked.

I enthusiastically answered "Nope." It took them a while to get it through to me. After that my nickname was "Offside".

I have been asked if I was ever intimidated by the size of the hockey players. At my first Portland Winter Hawks training camp, I counted 13 players who were 6'4" or more. Most of the other players

Audrey with Brent Bilodeau and Turner Stevenson at the Canadian Hockey League Allstar Game. Skates on or off, Audrey is usually the shortest player on the ice, but boy, can she skate!

were over 6'. The Winter Hawks were such a physically huge team that when I went to work with the Edmonton Oilers the pros actually seemed kind of small to me. Most players bend over at the waist to talk to me so I never really acknowledge being on the small side. Standing tall, I am almost 5-foot 4-inches. I do notice size when I work with a junior team and can look more than four players in the eyes. Then I say to myself, "I hope these guys are faster than the tough guys."

I now spend the year travelling worldwide, running schools and working with teams and organizations. They don't call me Offside any more.

INTRODUCTION

Power skating is a popular term for the application of basic skating techniques to the game of hockey. It is more than proper use of edges in a skating skill. Power skating has many components besides power. Balance, agility, flexibility, timing, rhythm, strength, control and energy expenditure all come together to produce coordinated and efficient movement.

Power skating has been a part of hockey for many years though it may not have been specifically referred to as such. Barclay Plager told me that when he was a player in the '60s and '70s with St. Louis, Eddie Shore used to make his team practice drills similar to the ones I teach.

Whenever a team has dominated the NHL, its style has been viewed as the successful mode to follow, imitate, develop and overtake. Skating has always been a part of the game but for the past decade has become the main focus and requirement of the game. The Edmonton Oilers dominated the scene for over ten years with their skating ability. As with teams of the past, like the Montreal Canadiens, opposing teams have had to adjust to the winning team's speed, ability and manoeuvrability in order to compete .

The game of hockey is not as simple as just going out and giving it your all. Whichever direction the game is moving in, the team and in particular, the player, must do whatever it takes to be successful. Many players take power skating instruction in order to enhance their game.

I have found that there are different levels at which players learn. Very few players can hear a description and immediately execute the skill. I know of a few players who can hear *and see* the skill, then execute it. There are players who can hear and see the drill, and then require part-by-part skill progression in order to execute it. And there are players who can hear, see, try part by part, yet still require manipulation by an instructor to set the position. Most hockey players fit into the last two categories. They learn the skill in progression and many require positioning assistance by the coach.

SLOW MOTION

Increased speed is a factor in skill breakdown. This is obvious to a player who moves up to a higher level of play — in particular from junior to professional. My approach to this is to rebuild specific skills — for example, the stride — using slow motion.

Skills are taught in slow motion to *set* the position not only physically but mentally. The brain lays down memory patterns every time a skill is performed. This is why it is so important to establish the correct position. It is easy to cheat or slide through a position when performing it quickly. To set and hold a position when going slow is much more difficult. Performing a drill slowly also makes it easier to analyze. Once the position is set then speed can be increased.

REPETITION

During a class I often tap the ball of my foot to the heel of the opposite foot, a return memory pattern. Most observers think I just have cold feet; well, sometimes I do. But mostly I am doing it because the brain remembers a *touch* position — where, for example, a part of your body makes contact with another part, or with your stick — longer than an *open* position. For example, under stress, during a stride the return of the released foot tends to become wider and wider. The knee does not bend as much for the next push, the full length of the muscle is not used, the muscles stay contracted and fatigue sets in quickly. The base becomes wider and wider and less effective. The touch position — bringing the released foot back to touch the other skate — must be repeated over and over, day after day, year after year.

Players often ask how many times they have to repeat a drill. I can never specifically answer that. It depends on their physical and mental capabilities. Let's just say that if you practice a skill 32 times in a row, then, over time, doing it once will be very easy.

Repetition is the key to establishing a position so that eventually it does not break down to the point of affecting the player's game. Under stress you perform what you do most often or what you did last. This is why it is so important to repeat a skill correctly in practice and not settle for making a mistake or performing so-so.

Because timing and rhythm are also essential to basic movement, I use music to set the tempo of the drills in my program. Music also helps to break the monotony of repetition. Repetition is necessary not only to develop technique but also to build cardiovascular and strength endurance during the drills.

MUSCLES

Many players are surprised at how physically demanding the drills are. I have intentionally tried to develop drills different from the usual hockey drills. This is to arouse the players' interest in their skating as well as to develop muscles the player does not normally use. Having a greater number of muscles to draw from will lengthen the life of the major muscle groups that are always used. Fine motor control requires players to be more in tune with how their bodies work. The step-by-step progression of skills in this book is designed to do just that.

In order to hold the body up structurally when going slow, the muscles work very hard and, without realizing it, the players are toning and conditioning their muscles. Therefore you extend the potential length of your career by drawing on a greater number of muscles and using the overused major muscle groups less.

The aim of technique training is to perform on demand. I would add that the goal is also to perform without thinking about the skill so you can concentrate on the game around you. One of my favourite sayings is: SKATE FROM THE HIPS DOWN AND PLAY HOCKEY FROM THE HIPS UP!

Skill training and fine motor control training require concentration without the stress factors that will cause them to break down during the season. These stress factors include the usual stresses that affect performance during the game and season: too many games in a week, speed, fatigue, injury, school commitments, team commitments, coaches, parents, fans, etc.

Therefore the summer is a good time for the player to focus just on skating skills. It is very important to keep learning technique in perspective. Skills are rarely accomplished immediately, yet a lot of players think that one week of power skating or hockey school is enough for their hockey career. I have had some players attend my school for ten years, not because they are slow learners but because they start to plan their own accomplishments for very specific skating skills and realize how many years it takes. I have a three-year plan for players to accomplish most of my program.

A player has a tremendous amount of information to process, perform and sustain throughout the season. Maintenance of power skating skills during the season is important. Most players find they need a refresher during the season, usually after 10 to 12 games. A two- or three-day refresher for the team gives them a break from the usual practice and gives the coach a break from the players!

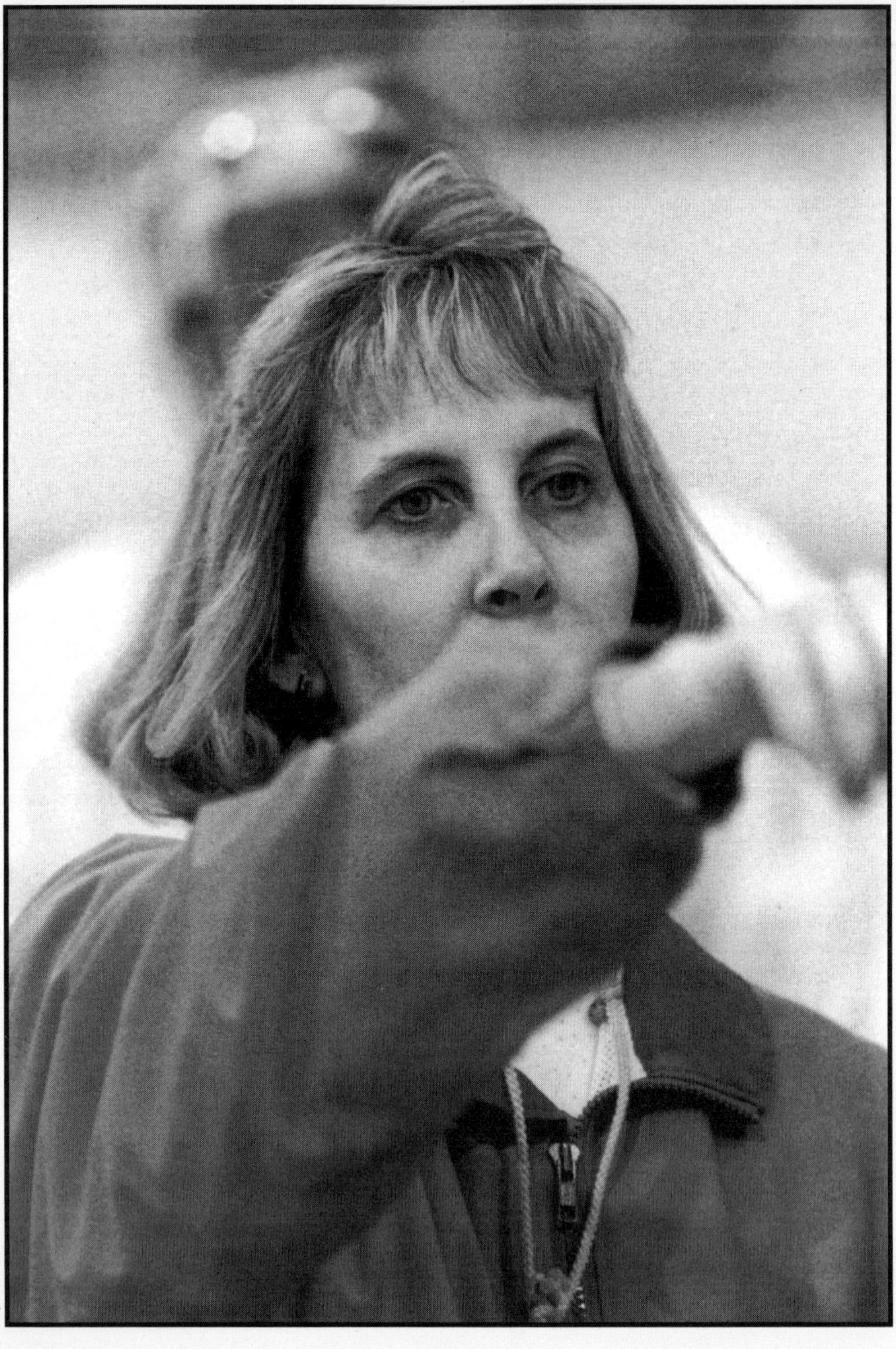
C. J. RELKE

A NOTE ON YOUR HOCKEY STICK

This book is designed in progression — one skill leads to the next. The same progression applies to the use of a hockey stick. Initially, use your hockey stick to establish your upper body balance: hold it in a horizontal position, hands shoulder-width apart, palms down (1). Then move your stick into a playing position (2), and eventually add the puck to as many drills as possible — even warm-up drills such as the Knee Raise.

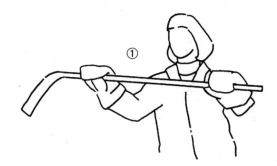

A NOTE ON MUSCLES

I make reference to a number of muscles and muscle groups throughout this book. It's a good idea for you to know and understand which exercises and stretches are using which muscles. This diagram will give you an idea of the approximate location of the major muscle groups that you make use of in power skating. After your first few hard practices, you may have a better ideas of where they are located.

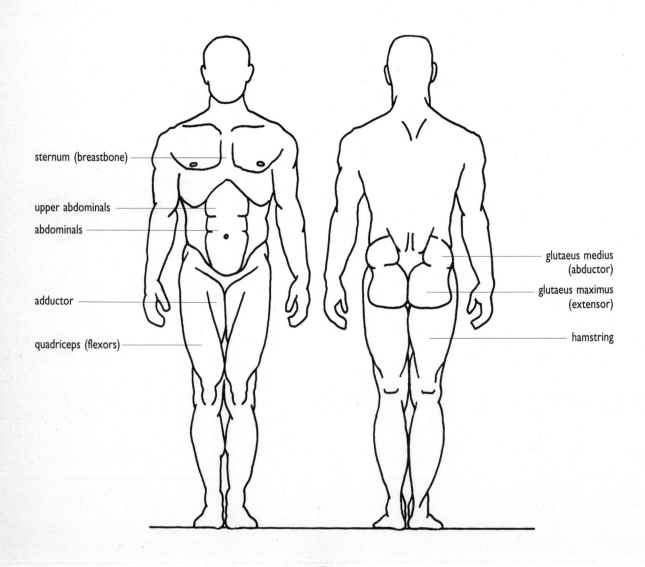

sternum (breastbone)

upper abdominals

abdominals

adductor

quadriceps (flexors)

glutaeus medius (abductor)

glutaeus maximus (extensor)

hamstring

A NOTE ON BASICS

BASIC STANCE

The Basic Stance is the starting point for many of the drills in this book. I base the stance on hip width — the feet are placed hip-width apart. Some instructors base it on shoulder width, but I teach so many junior and professional players with such a large shoulder width that this is not a realistic method. As well, I teach all lower body movement from the hip area, so the hip-width stance works best.

   Your knee should bend forward in line between your big toe and second toe. The inside of the knee should never fall or angle inside the ankle bone (knock-kneed) or outside the outside ankle bone (bow-legged). Your knee and blades should be perpendicular to the ice. I prefer a knee-bend that reaches not just over the toe but past the toe.

ADD THE PUCK

With any drill, at the point that you feel you have the sufficient balance and rhythm, you can add the puck. Even if you are not fully coordinated, you might try adding the puck if it tends to relax you. The timing and movement of the puck action often aids the skill movement.

REVERSE

Almost every drill in this book can be performed backwards as well as forwards. If you are comfortable with a skill in one direction, try reversing it and working on the other direction.

The staff at the Corral in Calgary were astonished that a female coach was running a hockey practice, and were upset because there was construction in the arena and there was no dressing room for me. I said "No problem, I can just use a cubbyhole under the stairs and the zamboni hose for a shower." After practice, I was heading for the zamboni to wet my towel down and the staff just about lost it because they thought I was really going to shower there!

•

Arena staff were not the only people who had to adjust to a female in hockey. Once when the Oilers were on the road, I had to run practice for the players left at home. We dressed at the Coliseum and then climbed into the team van to drive over to the practice rink. I climbed in and Ricky Morris, one of the old time vets, exploded, "I can handle the earrings, lipstick and perfume but nylons in hockey skates has got to go!" I started wearing sweat socks.

•

I've noticed that at most places I work, my restaurant and hotel meals keep getting bigger and bigger. I can lose up to ten pounds during training camp, so I guess the chefs decide to try and fatten me up. The players always notice my meals are bigger than theirs and soon also realize that I do not eat very much. So they start to vie to go with me for a meal. A dinner for three is more like one-and-a-third portion for them. The players usually feel guilty and end up buying my dinner. Barclay Plager eventually caught on and proclaimed, "Audrey is the only one in the NHL making money on meal money!"

WARM - UP

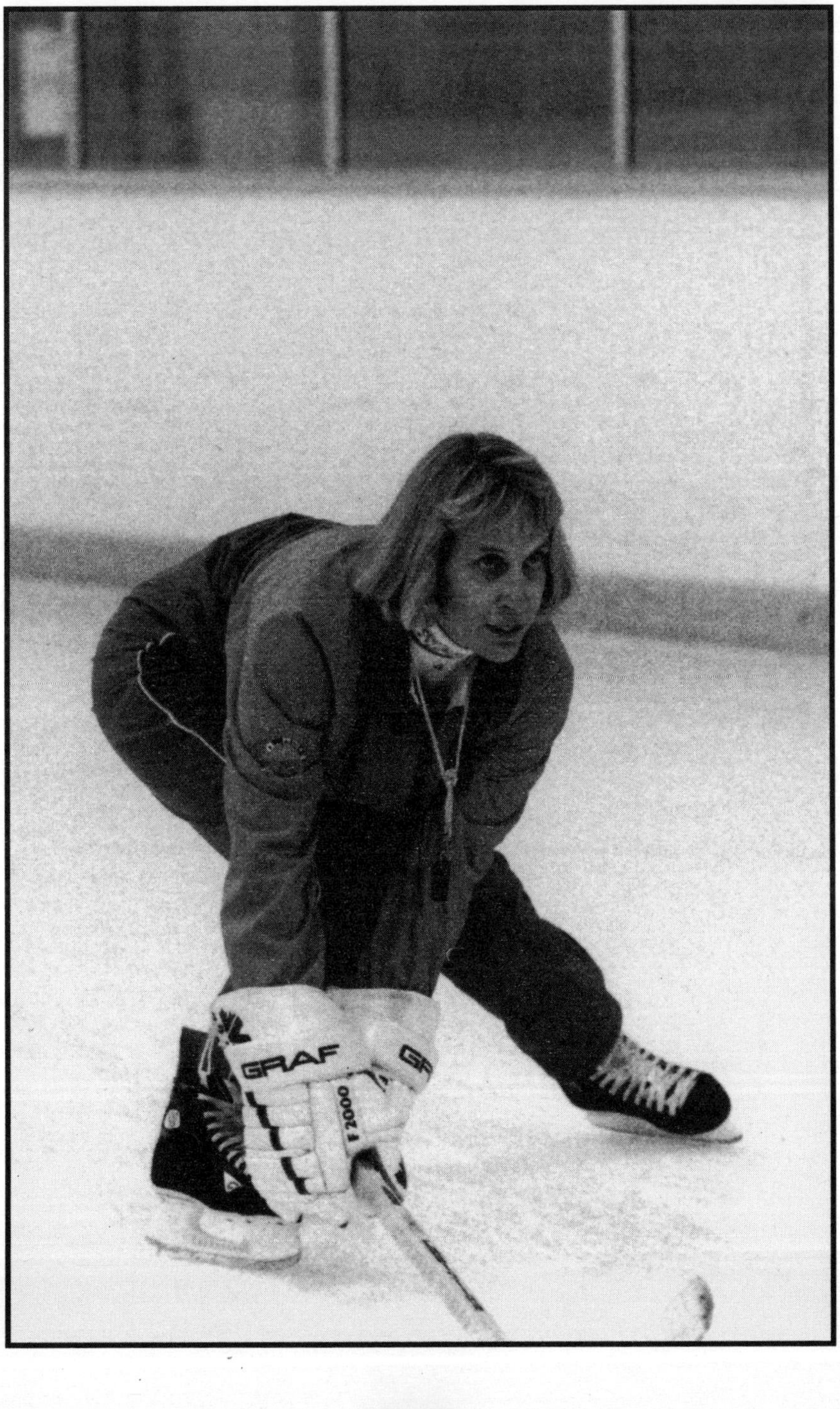

GRAF
F 2000

C. J. RELKE

WARM-UP

The Warm-up will stretch the full length of each muscle, from insertion point to insertion point, and move it through its full range of motion.

For most of these drills, skate fast around the end of the ice so that you gain enough momentum to maintain the drill the entire length of the ice. If you have a chance to skate around the ice a few times before starting Warm-up, your muscles will perform better and stretching will be easier than if you start out with "cold," tight muscles.

KNEE RAISE

The Knee Raise is used to warm-up the hip flexor muscles.

Raise and lower your knee five times as you glide down the length of the ice (1). Lift slowly — do not jerk your leg up and down.

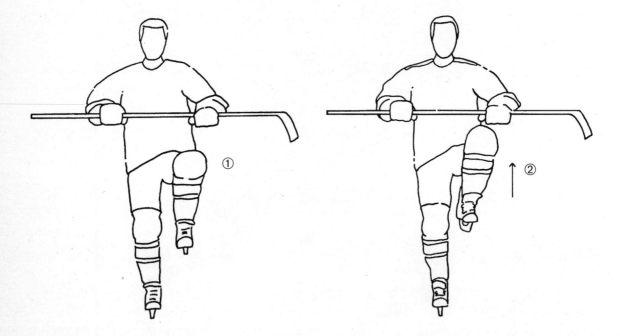

If you lift your knee higher than your hip (2), this drill will also stretch the gluteal muscles.

HIP OPENER

The Hip Opener is used to warm up your hip joint and stretch the groin.

Starting from the Knee Raise position (1), open your knee to the side and pull it back as far as possible. Tuck your heel in close to the skating knee (2). Open and close your knee slowly at least five times while gliding down the length of the ice.

CRANSTON SIT

The Cranston Sit is named after champion figure skater Toller Cranston because it is similar to a move he used in many of his freestyle programs.

The Cranston Sit is designed to stretch the groin and turn out the hip joint. Hip turn-out is essential for many skating skills.

Again, start from the Knee Raise position. Place your heel on your skating knee (1). Turn out and flatten the knee as far as possible. Keep your upper body posture erect. Use your abdominal muscles to stabilize your upper body and to avoid low back strain. Glide straight up the ice holding as deep a knee-bend as possible (2).

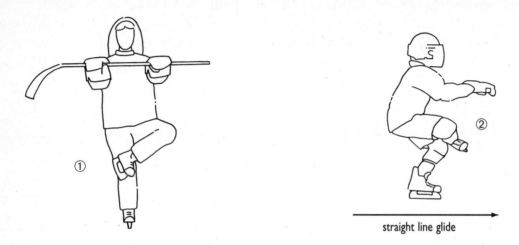

straight line glide

This drill can also be used to tone up and condition your quadriceps if you slowly move in and out of a Knee Bend while gliding in a straight line.

weave glide

This drill can improve balance and agility by changing the straight-line glide to a weave (3). Use knee-bends on each curve of the weave.

FRONT LEG LIFT

The Front Leg Lift stretches your hamstring muscles and strengthens your hip flexors. To fully stretch your calf muscles, you must point your toes toward your shin.

Lift your leg as high as you can, keeping it slightly bent until it is at the level you want (1). Then fully extend your leg.

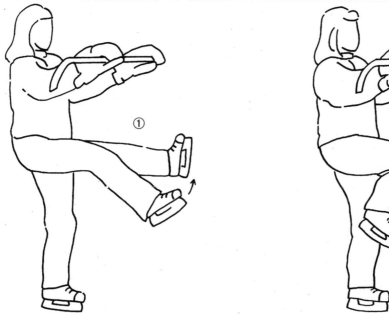
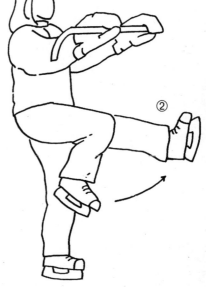

Variation: Do a Knee Raise first, then push your heel out to a full Leg Lift (2). Hold the position as long as possible without allowing your leg to bend or drop.

Always raise and lower your leg slowly, with control. Do not throw your leg up into position as the force or velocity of the movement can cause muscle strain.

SIDE LEG LIFT

The Side Leg Lift can be done two ways:

Lift your leg with your toes pointing up (1). This stretches the hip flexors.

Variation: Do the Hip Opener first, and then extend your foot out to the side.

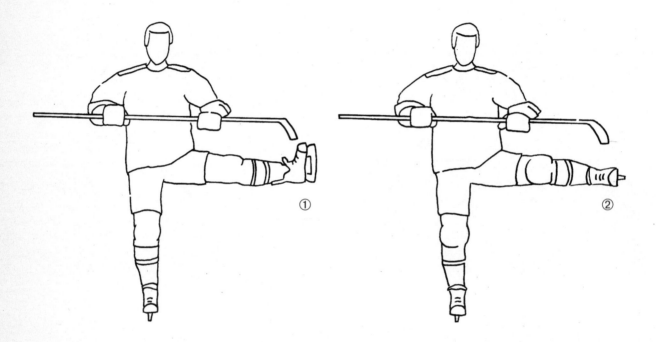

Position your toes horizontal to the ice, facing front (2). When done with control, this drill makes use of your outside leg muscles — the abductors — to lift, and your inside leg muscles — the adductors — to lower.

For conditioning purposes, hold the extension for the length of the ice.

BACK LEG LIFT

Push out to a full stride position, then slowly raise and lower your back leg. Turn your big toe out at least 90°, so that it is parallel to the ice, in order to exercise the abductors and gluteal maximus.

Remember, as always, to stabilize your upper body with your abdominals.

FRONT - SIDE - BACK LEG ROTATION

This combination drill will help develop effective hip turn-out.

Hip rotation in many players is limited. It is essential to have good hip turn-out, particularly for defensemen who must break from backward skating to forward, to chase after speeding wingers.

The Front-Side-Back Leg Rotation combines the three previous drills in one movement, and opens your hip joint to its maximum. When opening out, it is important to keep your leg at the same level, even if that means only raising your leg to knee level. You can eventually work up to hip level. Your knee should remain fully extended when rotating.

Front Leg Lift

Side Leg Lift

Back Leg Lift

Full Stride Position

End this drill by extending into a full stride position.

Variation: Reverse the rotation direction, Back-Side-Front.

BACK GROIN STRETCH

The Back Groin Stretch will stretch the groin of the extended leg.

Keep your upper body erect and gradually lower into a lunge position with the support knee in a full knee-bend over or past your skating toe (1). Try to drop your centre of gravity straight down while your back leg is turned out and extended back as far as possible (2).

Many players lean over their knee when doing the Back Groin Stretch. This actually limits the groin stretch because it tilts your pelvis up and forward. Instead, use your abdominals to stabilize your upper body. This way the centre of gravity can lower onto the ice equally between your legs, allowing your groin to stretch further.

Variation: Add a balance factor by raising a stick over your head and dropping your head back while gliding (3).

The veterans always treated me very well. Al Hamilton of the Oilers even let me wear his shin pads to scrimmage — he had shin pads that were smaller than usual. I now think it was probably a good excuse for him to get off the ice. Al, like most of the married players with kids, would occasionally bring his two children to practice. He used to help them do up their skates and I would give him a hard time about how important it was that they learn to put on their own skates and tie them up themselves.

Then, of course, a new pair of skates for me arrived from Bauer. They were so stiff and strong I could barely lace them, never mind tie them up. Doug Hicks came out early and offered to help me with my skates. I felt about five years old as he tied up my laces. Doug was just tying up my first skate when Al Hamilton came out early. As he skated past he yelled, "Hey Audrey, it's about time you learned to tie up your own skates!" I guess I deserved it.

FLAT - FOOTED SKATING

C. J. RELKE

FORWARD FLAT - FOOTED SKATING

Flat-footed Skating is gliding on the inside edges of both blades simultaneously. Your feet are as wide apart as possible and the extended leg should be straight (1). Use your abductor and quadricep muscles to perform a lateral weight shift — the shift should be to the side on which the puck is carried. The knee-bend is directly in line with the toe and pushing past the toe. As the weight shifts over to the side, shift from the inside edge to the flat of the blade (3). Both knees should bend at the midway point of the lateral shift (2).

Advanced Variation: [see next page] Sweep the puck in an arc as far back as possible on your forehand (1), keeping both hands on the stick (2). Then sweep all the way around — 180° — (3) in front to the backhand side (4), then complete the arc for a full 360°. On the backhand side, in order to reach around behind you will probably have to release the lower hand on the stick (5), but you should have two hands on the stick when you return to the forehand position. Keep your knee-bend to the side of the stick — both knees should be bent when you are at the 180° position (3).

  Your body should keep facing forward while your head turns to follow the puck, and your hips should stay square. Practice on the red line so you have a straight-line guide — keep your upper body perpendicular to the line. Advanced skaters should try to remain on the flat of the skate blade on the puck side when sweeping the puck behind the body. Try not to roll over on the outside edge. This variation calls for excellent upper-body flexibility.

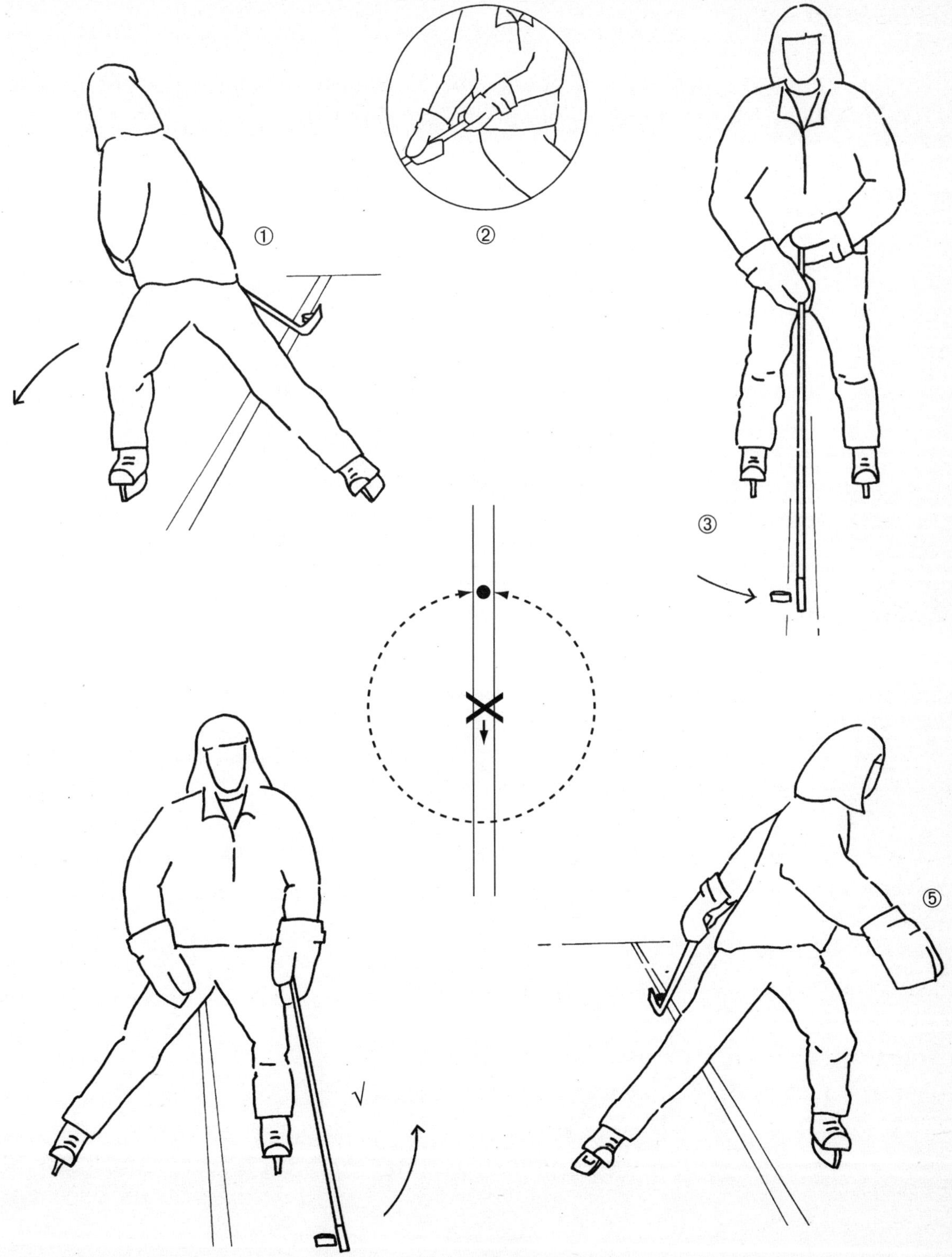
①
②
③
⑤

UPPER BODY TWIST

From the hips down, use the Flat-footed Skate (1). Rotate your upper body to the side of the knee-bend (2) to work on upper body flexibility (3).

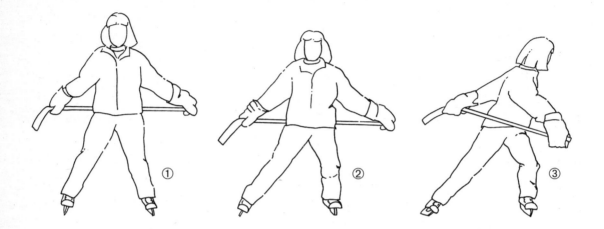

WINDMILL REACH

This is an excellent drill for stretching the back. The Windmill Reach adds upper body diagonal stretching to the lateral shifting of your lower body.

  Your lower body does the lateral shift of body weight. Your upper body is stretching diagonally — hand to opposite toe. Switch sides.

To stretch the back even more, rather than just touching your opposite hand to toe, reach forward ahead of the toe as far as you can.

LATERAL (OR SIDE) GROIN

The Lateral Groin is another variation of Flat-footed Skating. It involves a lateral shift in a full squat position.

Keep your feet the same distance apart throughout the shift. Again try to stay on the inside edges and keep your toes in line with each other horizontally. Bend down with your chest over your thigh. Keep your gloves on the ice. Push the support knee well past the toe so that one leg is in a full squat position during the lateral shift to that side (1). The other leg should be fully extended to the side. During the transfer both legs are in a full squat until the lateral shift is complete and the extended leg is straight (2). Use your abductor and quadricep muscles to shift laterally.

This drill emphasizes stretching the whole length of the muscle — insertion to insertion at either end of each muscle. This drill should not be attempted before you have done a few warm-up drills or you run the risk of straining a muscle. It should be done with a controlled amount of speed so that your momentum transfers to the shifting action.

TWO - FOOT SKIING (SLALOM)

Whenever possible, I like to relate skating to another sport. This gives the drill another dimension, and sometimes takes your mind off what you are doing — just let your body go. With this drill, imagine yourself downhill skiing.

Many players gouge the ice when they skate flat-footed or two-foot ski. This may create the illusion that you are working hard, and may make the ice appear that you have had a tough practice, but you may just be wasting a lot of effort. Many people are intrigued by the fact that I know how well a team or player skates by listening to the amount of noise they produce while skating. Skating *with* the ice rather than against it saves energy, maintains momentum and includes the element of surprise — your opponent may not hear you coming. This is a difficult concept to explain, but think of it in terms of anticipation — you are already moving ahead to the next move or step. Think of skimming the ice surface and being as light as possible. The ice will stay in better condition during your practices as well.

Two-Foot Skiing is like doing moguls — your upper body faces square, your hips move out to the side, and your knee-bend is deep. Try rolling over the four edges effortlessly and pull the ice up into the next curve. As well, try to separate your upper body from your lower body. The upper body should remain centered and the lower body should ski out to the sides. Keep your stick straight ahead.

This drill can be divided into three bases or tracks: Wide, Basic and Narrow. These three tracks are used for many of the drills throughout this book.

wide track

For the Wide track, keep your feet in the Basic Stance while trying to ski as far to the side as possible. Or, alternatively, keep your feet as wide as possible and roll over all four edges on a very wide track. This is a balance drill that works on lowering your centre of gravity while maintaining control. The Wide track emphasizes stretching.

The Basic track uses the same width base as in the Basic Stance. Your feet are hip width apart. The knee-bend is over and past the toe and the track is wider. This base is used to develop power.

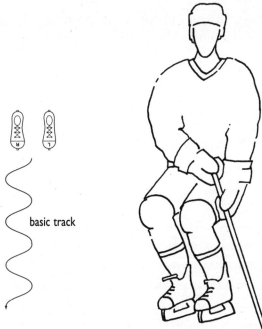

basic track

The Narrow track is used to improve agility. Keep your feet and legs together and your knees bent past your toes (1). Ski as fast as possible. Create a very tight track.

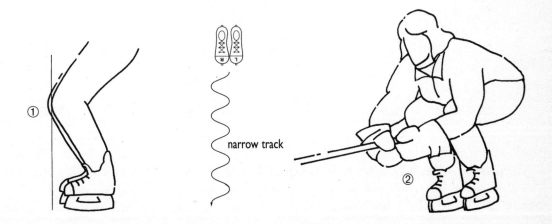

narrow track

Variation: For conditioning and balance, practice Two-Foot Skiing in a full squat (2).

IN AND OUT (SCULLING)

The technical name for In and Out is Sculling. This is the perfect drill for developing your abductor muscles. In and Out involves drawing a half-circle with each foot which join to make a full circle. This movement is performed while travelling in a straight line. Again, three bases are used: Wide, Basic and Narrow.

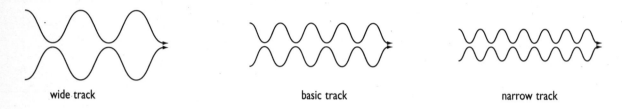

wide track   basic track   narrow track

The Wide base is again used for stretching. This In and Out can be done in a variety of ways. Beginners should keep your upper body erect (1) and let your body weight stretch your legs out as far as possible (2), and then pull your legs back in until your toes tap together (3). The in-and-out action should always end with the toe tap to ensure your whole muscle length is used.

Variation — Legs Together: Bend over at the waist and try to touch your forehead to your knees with your legs together (1, next page). Extend your stick horizontally behind your back and below your rear-end on the out (2), and down by your ankles as you lower your forehead to your knees (1). This is a tough drill on your back so be sure to do a few back bends to relieve the back muscles.

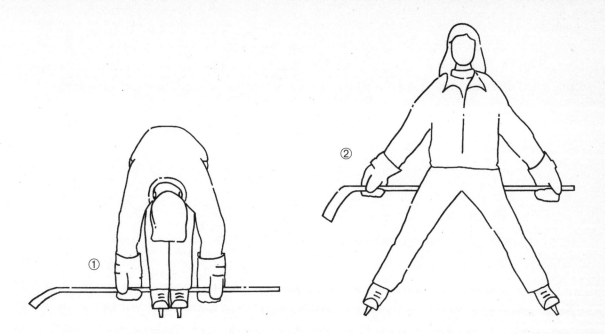

Variation — Legs Apart: Hold your stick behind your back, at rear-end level on the In (1, below). On the Out movement, your stick is behind your back and extended down as close to the ice as possible (2). Bend your upper body forward while pulling your head toward your knees.

Variation — Upper Body Stretch: Add a forward upper body stretch. On the Out glide, carry your stick horizontally in front of your body, stretch your wrists (or elbows, if you are really flexible) to the ice and reach forward. This really stretches the insertions of the hamstrings and should be done with a controlled amount of speed.

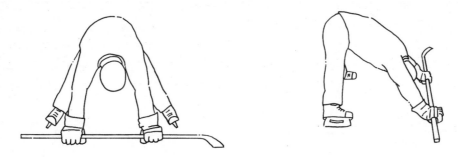

The Basic track is used for power training because in this stance the knee-bend can be at its maximum, even in the Out position. Push your feet out to hip width using the inside edges (1), then pull them back together using your adductor muscles (2).

Variation: For conditioning and balance, practice the In and Out in a Basic Stance in a full squat (3).

A Narrow track is used for agility training. Keep your feet about two inches apart and tap your toes together as fast as possible (4).

PUMPING (ONE - FOOT SCULLING)

Pumping is doing an In and Out on a curve with the outside foot (1) while the inside foot glides along (2). Most instructors teach pushing back on the pump out. I prefer pushing *horizontally* out and then *pulling* up the ice until the toes are even and touching together.

Because it is a flat-footed skill, both skate blades stay on the ice. On the curve, the outside foot doing the in-and-out action is on the inside edge (1). The inside foot is on the flat of the blade (2). The gliding knee (inside foot) has maximum knee-bend (2) as the outside foot is pumping as far out to the side as possible.

With effective pumping, you will be able to maintain movement on a curve. When pumping backwards, pull your *heels* together to finish the pump.

Make sure that you do not ignore a skill because you think you don't need it to play your position. I believe that forwards should be able to skate as well backwards as the defense can. The defense should have as strong a stride as the forwards. At my school, most drills are done forwards and backwards, except for one drill in particular. The problem is, I usually forget which drill it is until a player tries it and struggles.

I was working for the Calgary Flames and had forward and defense sessions. My challenge to the defense was that they had to improve their stride to the point that they could out-skate the forwards. My challenge to the forwards was that they had to skate backwards without any indication that they played forward. The key was to fly into a backward position without hesitation.

As my camps progress, the players do rounds of warm-up. Each round is a different skill — the challenge is to build speed as the rounds go on rather than slowing due to fatigue. The forwards had a handle on this concept to the point that I could just watch the warm-up and sip on a coffee. Brett Hull was leading the pack and I was thinking, "Boy, is he ever fast today." Just then I realized he was about to turn backwards into the drill you could not do backwards.

Before I could get my whistle up, he had whipped backwards, tried the drill and the shocked look on his face sent me into howls of laughter. I finally managed to blow the whistle and admitted to Brett we should skip that drill. Each summer at my school we have the Best Face of the Summer award. The player who produces the best expression during a drill wins. Brett won the Best Face of the Summer award. Actually, no one has outdone him since.

BACKWARD SKATING

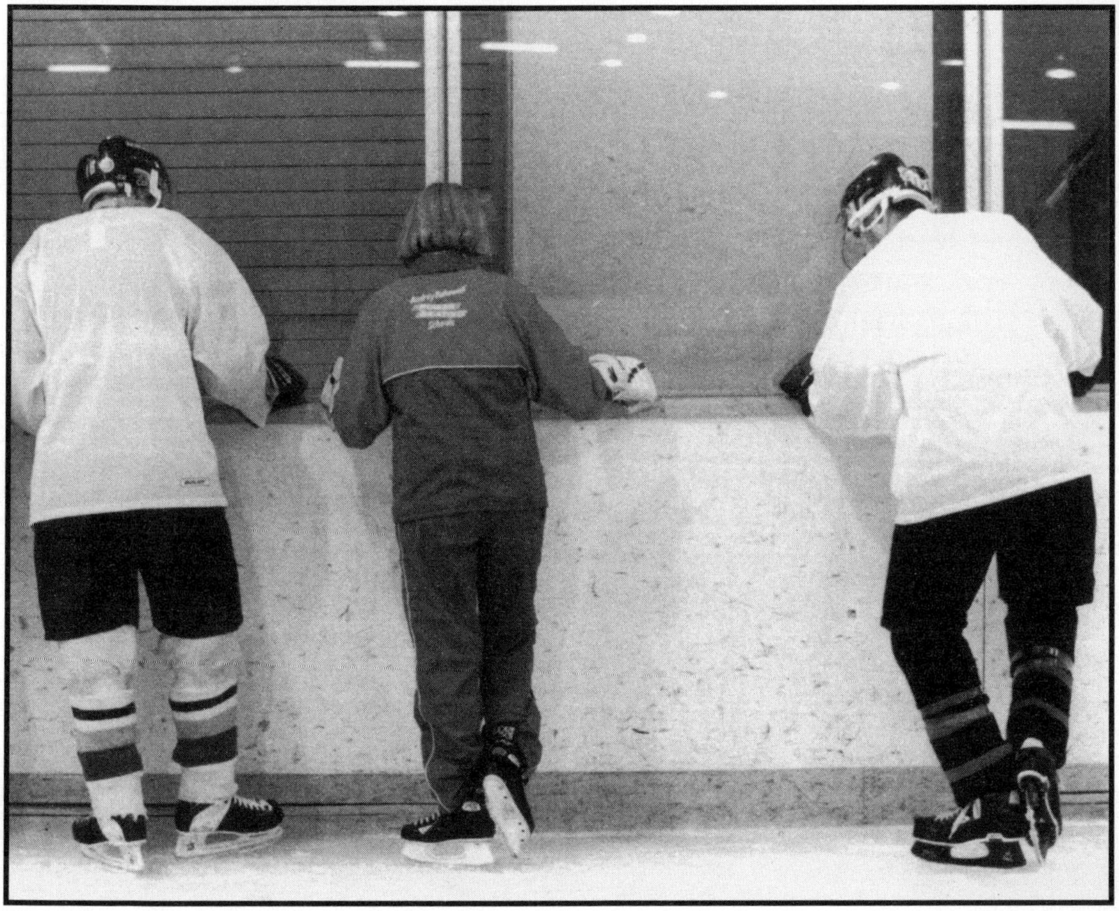

C. J. RELKE

BACKWARD SKATING

When first learning to skate backwards, players often try pushing themselves off from the boards and then wiggle their behinds. This method causes the player to start off unbalanced since bending the arms into the boards for a good push causes the upper body to lean forward — the centre of gravity is forward instead of being under the body and Boom! the blades slide out behind the body.

When first learning Backward Skating, use a partner and your hockey sticks for support. Tuck your sticks in close to your hips in order to eliminate swinging (1). Start off walking backwards with your feet parallel to the sticks.

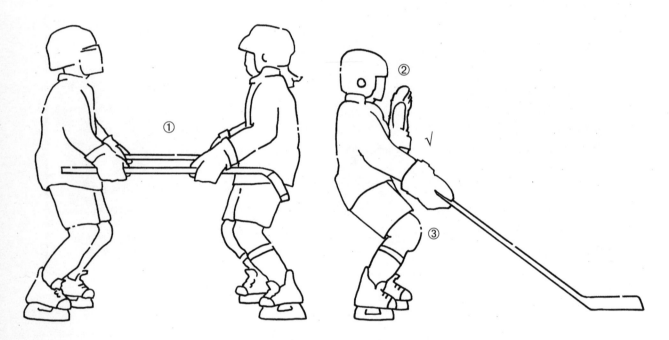

DEFENSIVE SIT STANCE

The Defensive Sit Stance is the same as the Basic Stance — the feet are hip width apart. The key to this stance is posture. The abdominals stabilize the upper body and your head is up, allowing for good peripheral vision (2). In your mind, create a balance box in your abdominal region (from the bottom of the sternum to about two inches below your navel. This box is the upper body support system and must not collapse. If it does the trunk tilts forward, your knees straighten and you will be crunched forward, finding movement very awkward or asking yourself if you were a zamboni in a previous life. To create a good balance box, imagine short sticks as your side supports — every time you break forward you are poked by the stick. Or have your coach gently poke you to see if your abdominal muscles are soft — they should be firm to touch. Advanced players can also try tucking your abdominal muscles in toward your spine.

Remember to keep breathing. It sounds funny, but try this: sit up straight and tuck your upper abdominals in. Held your breath, didn't you? Better practice this a few times before trying it on the ice. By the way, did you notice that when you tucked in your abdominals your chest expanded a bit? This method also helps to make you look bigger to your opponent — always an advantage.

Now that your upper body is under control, tuck your hips under your body. This means you will line up your rear-end (where the cheek joins the leg) with the heels of your skates. As always, make sure your knee-bend is directly over and past the toe (3). Extend your stick in front and hold the released hand up in front for balance (4). Follow your opponent with the palm of your hand and your fingertips. Use the palm of this hand to aid in your feel for balance as well as having it ready for defensive use such as pushing away an opponent.

   To start, push straight down into the ice keeping your feet hip-width apart and under your body. Try shifting your weight very slightly from one foot to the other. When in trouble, try to return to the Defensive Sit Stance. It is the most stable position when skating backwards.

C - CUT

The C-Cut is the most common method used in teaching Backward Skating. It is like drawing the letter C or a half-circle in the ice. I avoid this method because players tend to not maintain the established base during the pull backwards. Instead, they start to lose their balance by turning the toe inward to start the C, and then swing to pull the feet back to a straighter, more comfortable position. Then they panic, the hips go back and Boom! game over. If anything, I suggest pushing straight down into the ice and skating as straight a path backwards as possible with the feet a little wider than the Basic Stance. The toes point straight ahead while you use a *shallow* C-Cut.

   I do use the C-Cut for more advanced players who may use it for starting off backwards, although I always prefer staying square to the opposition. If you must use it, when alternating C-Cuts, keep your weight over the balance knee rather than the pushing leg. For example, if your right leg is pulling, anchor your left leg like a pivot and rotate around it in the basic stance. By the end of the pull, transfer your weight over to your right foot. Skaters using this method should keep their weight anchored right in the middle between your feet during the pull. Your feet should stay the same distance apart — balance goes haywire when they get too close together.

Try the same bases as with Forward Two-footed Skating: Wide, Basic and Narrow.

WIDE   BASIC   NARROW

The Wide track is with very little scull or C-Cut action — your feet are as wide apart as possible and your pushes are short and quick. The Basic track is hip width apart, pretty much the same as the Defensive Sit. The Narrow track is again for agility. Your feet and legs press together and the ski action is tight and quick.

BOOM BOOM DRILL

The Boom Boom Drill is the best method for teaching backwards skating to beginners.

The Boom Boom Drill is a variation of the Basic Stance. Keep your feet hip width apart and swing your hip out as far to the side as possible, just like doing the Bump (kids — it was a dance in the '70s — ask your parents for a demo). Your upper body does not shift to the side — only your hip does. Your upper body remains squared up and stays centred. This drill is a lead-up to a lateral shift because it shifts your hip to the side as far as it can go. When shifting laterally, the hip must line up over the support skate — a straight line should run through shoulder, hip and ankle.

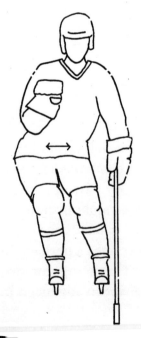

Initially start doing this drill on the spot. Keep your feet hip-width apart or use the hockey lines for a visual guide to stance width. Work the Basic Stance, hips and knee-bend, then try it while moving backwards around the ice. I find that the hip action is so amusing that players forget about going backwards. The hip action transfers the weight and creates the movement.

Variation: A variation of the Boom Boom Drill is the Double Boom Boom Drill. This is the same as Boom Boom, except two Boom Booms are done to the same side. Most players can easily rotate their hips forward and backward but are limited in rotation to the side. This drill over-extends your hip to the side and makes you hold the position longer.

GLOVE DRILL

This glove-between-the-knees drill emphasizes proper stance width.

Often the base for Backward Skating is too narrow. Set your upper body in Defensive Stance with one hand on the stick and the stick extended in front. Take your glove off the other hand and hold it horizontally by the thumb. Bend your knees deep enough so that your glove is extended down between your knees (1). The space between your knees must be wider than the glove. Push straight down into the ice using the ball of your foot.

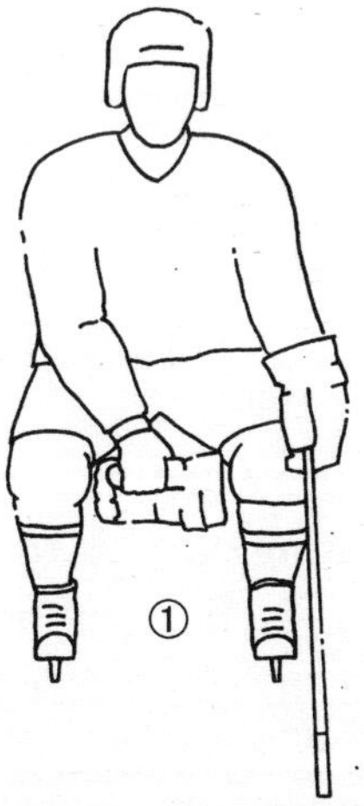
①

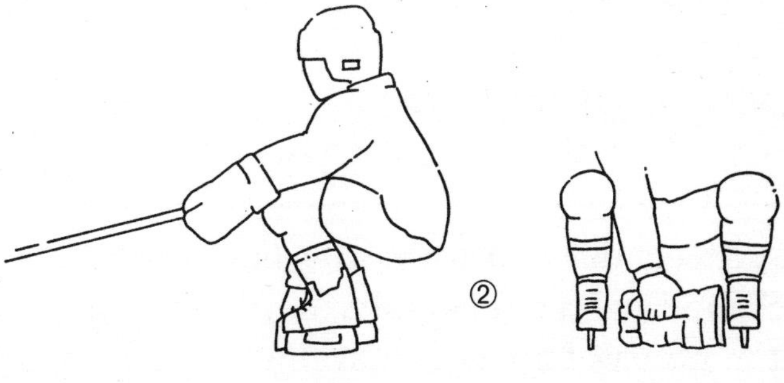
②

Variation: Do this drill in a full squat with your glove down, sliding along the ice (2).

FOOTBALL DRILL

This variation on a football drill will improve your agility and foot control.

In the Defensive Sit Stance, instead of just gliding backwards, do fast up-and-down steps, moving the feet laterally — wide and narrow — as fast as possible. It should look like you are running through a track of tires.

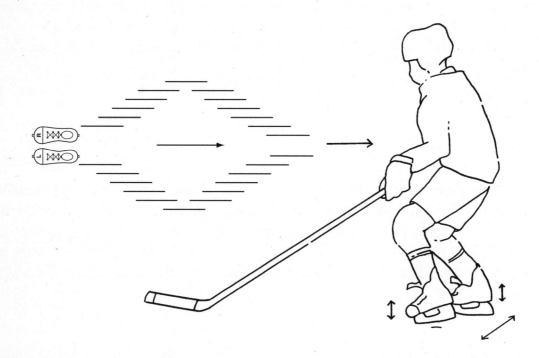

Variation: Do the Football Drill while travelling in a zigzag pattern rather than just straight backwards. This requires quick pushes from the ball of the foot.

BACKWARD LATERAL SHIFT

The Backward Lateral Shift is the same as the Lateral Shift in Forward Flat-Footed skating, except that you are moving backwards. It involves extending one leg from the Basic Stance into a full lateral extension, using the inside edges for control and the abductor muscles for lateral movement. Then shift the extension to the other leg.

This drill, which I like to refer to as the Paul Coffey Lateral Shift because he is the expert with this movement, is similar to the Lateral (Side) Groin stretch, except that you should be using a defensive upper body sit stance instead of a full squat. Your upper body remains square and your shoulders must remain level in order to avoid indicating to your opponent which side your weight has shifted to. A straight line should extend through the shift: shoulder, hip, knee, ankle. Keep your hand level and follow your opponent with your fingertips, and keep your stick extended, ready to poke-check or move into a playing position.

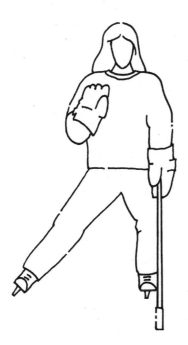

BACKWARD STRIDE

The Backward Stride with upper body twist is great for flexibility and balance. I call this the Mark Messier drill because of the follow-through with the elbows. From the hips up, twist and pull one elbow back as far as you can. Turn your head to look over and past your elbow. The foot on the side of the twist may slide back a bit to that side but will return to the Basic Stance during the transfer to the alternate side.

A few years ago, every time I went to Banff this tireless little kid would ask for extra ice time; he would move up with the older boys or help with the younger kids. In the spring, I would come to run an Evaluation Camp. He would be waiting to get some extra ice before the camp and would go on while I was there to set up the coach and scout room.

It would take me at least two hours to set up and every once in a while I would go up the ramp to see if he was practicing or fooling around. He never saw me watch — he would work the whole time: skate and shoot, skate, shoot, skate, dipsy doodle and on and on. In my room I could hear the puck hitting the boards. When I finished he was still at it. I always thought, that kid could make it. Today Ryan Smyth plays for the Edmonton Oilers.

EDGES

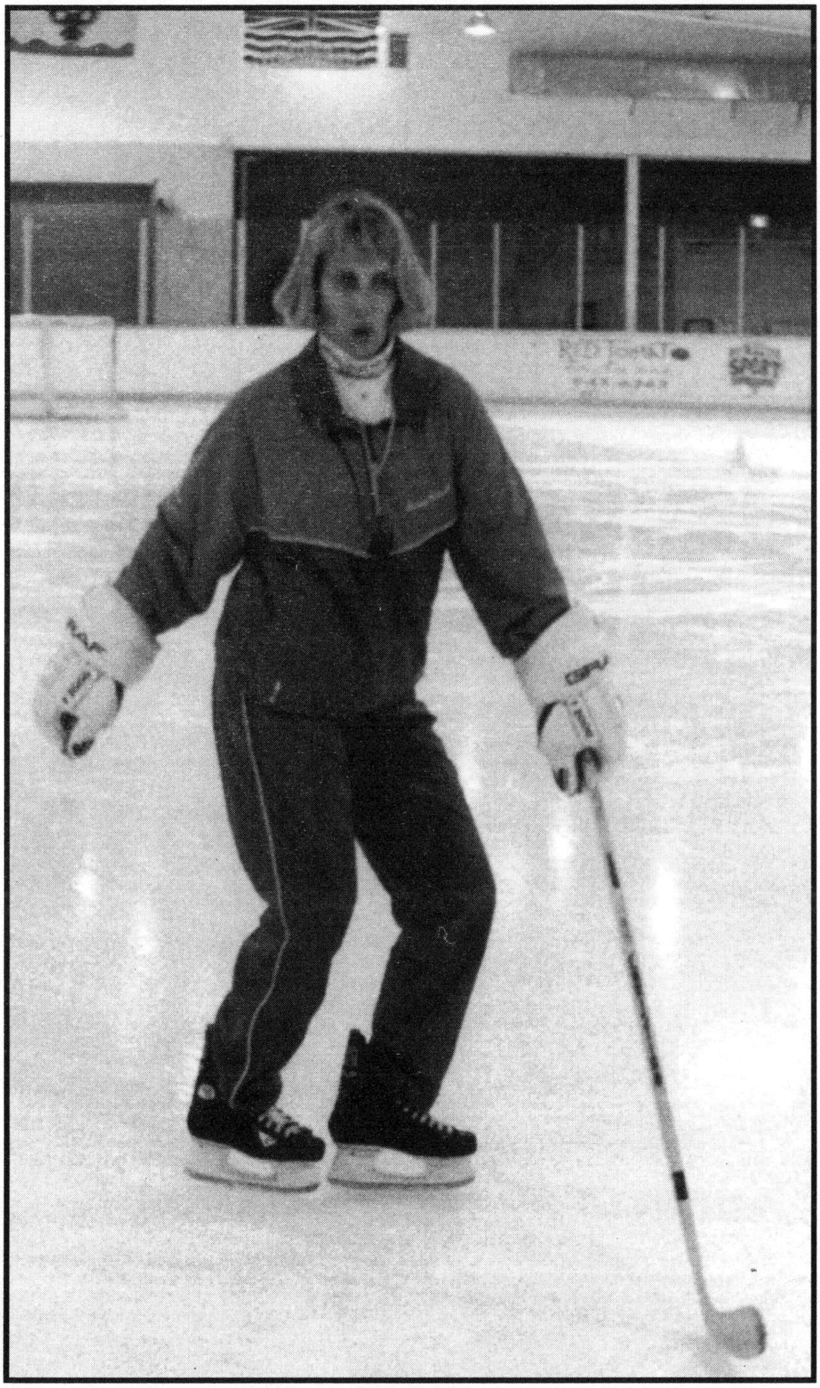

C. J. RELKE

EDGES

An effective skater uses four different edges — two going forward and two going backwards. If you lean to the inside of your foot, you are on the inside edge. If you pick up your inside foot while on a curve, you are on your inside edge. If you lean to the outside of the foot, you are on the outside edge; on a curve, if you pick up your outside foot, you are on your outside edge.

For a proper progression, I teach edge control in reverse order: the Return, the Curve, then the Start. The Return is first because in order to have an efficient push, a player must know where and how to return the released foot to the ice. In order to be ready for the transfer to the next step, the big toe of the released foot should return horizontally to the heel, and slide up the inside of the boot until your toes are even.

In practice, you want to achieve these exact positions because once you add speed, you automatically lose some of your positioning. Stress may occur in a number of ways during a game — from the game itself, the overwhelming plays, or the yelling of the coach, parents, or fans. Stress in a game situation can result in a break down of the learned position. The body tends to remember what it does most often or what it did last. Laying patterns in the brain is as important as training the muscles. If you watch good tennis players they always repeat the correct stroke after making a mistake. Always practice the perfect position; you will soon notice that in game situations your pushing ability has strengthened and your endurance is greater.

A good hip-width stance when skating slowly can develop into ineffective railroading when you are speeding up the ice. Railroading is something coaches and scouts watch for. It means that the striding base of a player is so wide that it resembles a railroad track. Especially when fatigued, a player's pushes can be so short and wide so that he rocks back and forth like a train, creating more horizontal movement than forward acceleration. Precise positioning avoids railroading.

FORWARD INSIDE — STEP TOUCH (THE RETURN)

The purpose of this drill is to practice both the proper return of your skate to the ice, and the preparation for the next stride.

Forward inside edges are the most-used edges in hockey. To make sure the return foot is fast and neat, begin with the Forward Step Touch drill. Step and tuck in the released toe to the skating heel. Alternate as you skate straight up the ice.

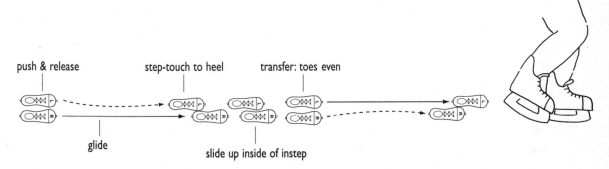

FORWARD INSIDE — AGILITY OR FISHTAIL EDGE (THE CURVE)

Control of the Agility Edge is essential for proper movement on a curve.

To begin working on inside edges, I like to use short edges with a quick curve. Some coaches call it a C-Cut, but as I mentioned earlier, I prefer to glide rather than to cut the ice, to skate with the ice rather than against it.

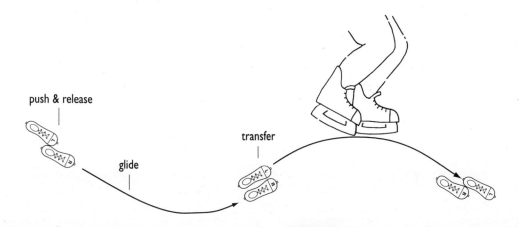

I call this the Agility or Fishtail Edge — fishtail, because the released foot reminds me of a fishtail. I like the foot to snap in under the body, and to stay at the heel following the curve until ready to move forward for the transfer. The player begins skating up the ice in Step Touch, and then starts to draw a curve toward the midline of the body with the stick. Emphasize rolling the stick blade from forehand to backhand — this will rotate your shoulders around the curve, creating a short, quick curve. This is a good method for beginners because they find the Technical Edge difficult to maintain. Start off short and then move up to the Technical Edge.

FORWARD INSIDE — TECHNICAL EDGE (THE START)

The Technical Edge Drill helps to develop control, emphasizing the proper push.

The Technical Edge is the inside edge used in figure skating. It is a 180° rotation or a half-circle. Use this drill to introduce total body control while travelling slowly, and to emphasize pushing using the ball of the foot. An actual line can be used as a visual aid to indicate when the half circle should end. The skater starts in a T or V push, carrying the stick horizontally. The stick is used to show balance and to stop over-rotation.

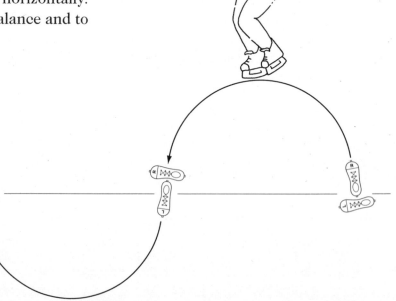

After takeoff, the released foot is tucked into the heel, the same position as for Step Touch and Fishtail. The knee-bend is deep and continuous. To change feet, your toe slides up your instep until the toes are even and a push with a 90° turnout is executed using the ball of the pushing foot. The 90° turnout is an indicator of hip flexibility rather than ankle flexibility. Players that have a wide stride stance should practice this turnout and the use of the ball of the foot because when railroading the push tends to be off the heel. Try to maintain the same speed throughout the edge. Keep a straight line, perpendicular to the ice, right down from the knee through to the skate blade. On any edge, do not allow the knee to fall inside or outside of the ankle bone.

Note: For maximum power, the ball of the foot should initiate the push.

FORWARD INSIDE — OVER - ROTATED INSIDE EDGE

The Over-Rotated Inside Edge is used for endurance and balance.

Push off on a big inside edge and keep rotating, trying to carry the edge in as close to a full circle as possible. Change feet when you feel like you are going to fall off the edge. Try to maintain the same speed throughout. Keep a straight line, perpendicular to the ice, right down from the knee through to the skate blade. Keep your knees bent and your toe tucked into the heel — emphasis is on upper-body rotation. On any edge, do not allow the knee to fall inside or outside of the ankle bone.

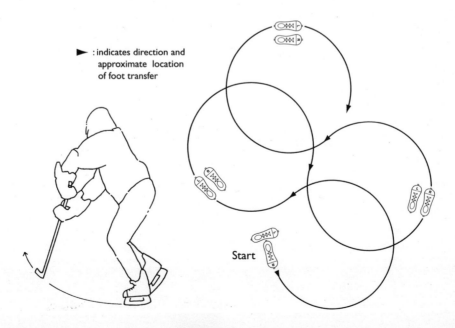

▶ : indicates direction and approximate location of foot transfer

Start

Variation: Use a partner following like a shadow one stick length behind the leader. Both partners start on the same edge at the same time. The leader rotates in a tight circle until he can tap his partner's stick behind him. Then he changes feet and rotates around to the other side and again taps his partner's stick.

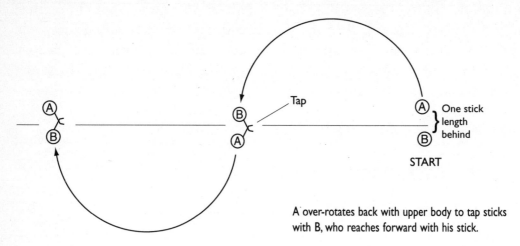

A over-rotates back with upper body to tap sticks with B, who reaches forward with his stick.

Once you have the timing established, add the puck and a short pass at the end of each arc.

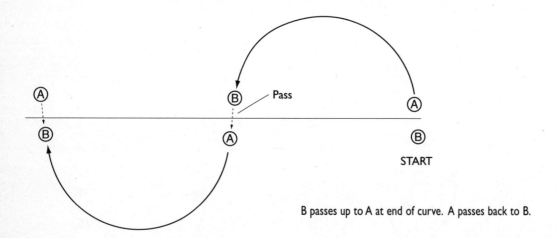

B passes up to A at end of curve. A passes back to B.

Variation: To double-check your inside edge control, set up a zigzag pylon course. Push off five feet before the first pylon. Hold the edge while looping all the way around the pylon and out toward the next pylon until you run out of steam and have to change feet. Only use one push between pylons.

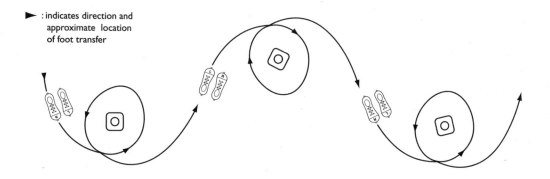

▶ : indicates direction and
approximate location
of foot transfer

FORWARD INSIDE — SPREAD - EAGLE

The Spread-Eagle is a glide on a curve in which both feet are on inside edges. It is used in hockey for sustaining movement and even for shooting. To further sustain movement, pump the back foot.

FORWARD OUTSIDE — TECHNICAL EDGE

As with the Inside Technical Edge, this Outside Technical Edge drill involves a 180° rotation, or a half-circle. I like using the outside Technical Edge because the change of feet and push-off is tricky. The released toe returns to the heel and slides up the instep until it is in line with the skating toe, ready to transfer. The push-off is more difficult because the ball of the foot can not dig in as easily as on the inside edge. As a result, the hip turnout is important — turn out as far as you can, and attempt to get a 90° turnout for the push.

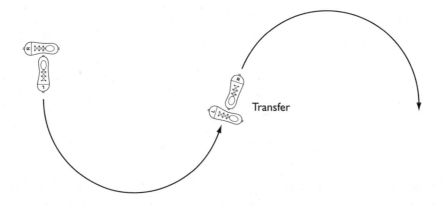

FORWARD OUTSIDE — OVER-ROTATED OUTSIDE EDGE

Push off on a big outside edge and keep rotating as close to a full circle as possible. Change edges when you feel like you are going to fall off the edge. During the transfer from one foot to the other on the Over-Rotated Edge, it is easy to do a crossover instead of a T or V push. The T or V requires more total body control. Remember: neat feet are fast feet.

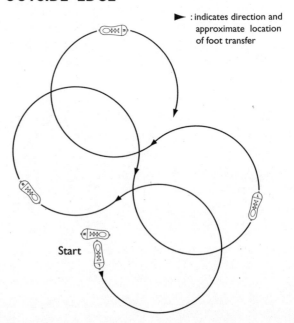

► : indicates direction and approximate location of foot transfer

Variation: Add a partner and try the shadow drill. First try the stick tap, then the puck pass (see page 56).

Variation: As you did with the inside edges, check your total body control by sustaining the outside edge while looping around a zigzag course of pylons.

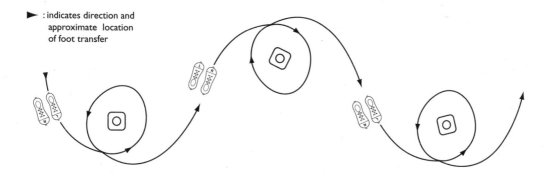

: indicates direction and approximate location of foot transfer

BACKWARD EDGES

To improve balance and agility, repeat the four edge drills backwards, starting with the Step Touch:

BACKWARD INSIDE — STEP TOUCH

Start off stationary, stepping to the side then standing on one foot momentarily while the other foot tucks in by the skating toe (toe touches toe). When you did the Forward Step Touch, you touched toe to heel. Going backwards, touch toe to toe because the released-foot action will be opposite to forwards. The released-foot action forward is heel-instep-toe whereas for backwards it is toe-instep-heel.

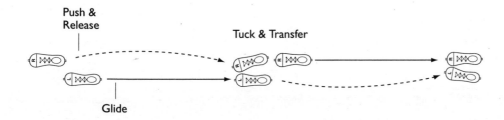

Push & Release

Tuck & Transfer

Glide

BACKWARD INSIDE — AGILITY OR FISHTAIL EDGE

Use short, tightly curved edges with quick transfer from one foot to the other. As the released foot draws from the toe to the instep to the heel, use it to help direct the curve of the edge. Allowing the released foot to swing wide away from the skating foot will cause you to fall inside the curve and lose the edge. Keep the released foot touching the heel until it steps down for the transfer.

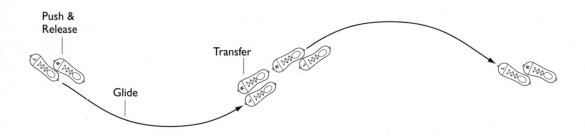

BACKWARD INSIDE — TECHNICAL EDGE

When practicing backward edges, inside or outside, it is important to have your rear-end leading the way. Remember to keep it tucked in.

The Backward Technical Edge is difficult for most hockey players to execute. The easiest method to practice is to set up a zigzag pylon course. Hold up your inside foot for as long as possible as you skate past the pylon. Emphasize the toe-instep-heel tuck. Upper body posture should be upright and your head should face into the curve.

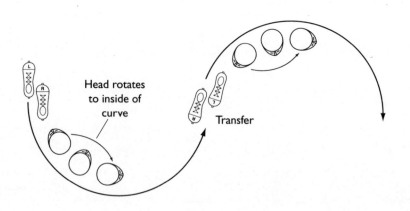

The Technical Edge for the advanced player indicates whether you are able to separate portions of your body and still maintain control. In other words, you should be able to skate the edge from the hips down with little assistance from the upper body.

First of all, use the same method as going forwards, carrying the stick horizontally to assist in upper body control. Again, use a line as a visual guide for when you should change feet. The arc should be a half-circle. The takeoff should be a back pump push with one foot transferring to the other foot to glide. An easier method is to skate backwards at the start of the curve, picking up the inside foot as soon as possible. The released foot must tuck in to the toe right away and then draw back to the instep and heel. As the released foot draws back, keep your knees together for better balance. Look to the inside of the curve to see where you should change feet. At the point of transfer, the gliding foot becomes the foot pushing into the next edge. Stay down on your knee and use the same action as in a Backward In and Out, remembering that you are on one foot. If this is too difficult, lower the released foot, skate backwards a bit and then pick up the inside foot on the opposite curve.

Try this drill carrying your stick in playing position, and then add the puck.

BACKWARD INSIDE — OVER - ROTATED INSIDE EDGE

Use the zigzag pylon course to test your ability to sustain the edge. Start off skating backwards. Approximately five feet before the pylon, pick up the inside foot and keep it tucked while you glide all the way around the pylon and out towards the next pylon. If possible, use only one pump push to change feet, otherwise skate backwards for a bit. Add the puck.

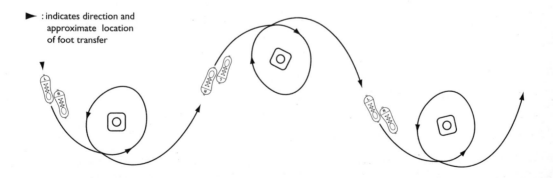

▶ : indicates direction and
    approximate location
    of foot transfer

BACKWARD OUTSIDE — TECHNICAL EDGE

Use a line as a visual guide for a half circle, and again use backward skating to get you moving. As soon as possible, pick up the outside foot on the circle and tuck that foot in for the toe-instep-heel draw. Keep your knees together. This time the body and head rotation is to the outside of the circle. Your upper body is erect and the stick is carried horizontally. When changing feet, the push-off is a back pump push the same as you did for the Backward Inside Technical Edge. If you have trouble balancing on one foot, then touch down and skate backward until you can pick up the outside foot on the opposite curve.

Once you have total body control, try this edge while carrying the puck.

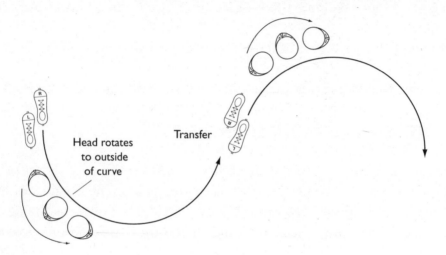

Head rotates to outside of curve

Transfer

BACKWARD OUTSIDE — OVER - ROTATED OUTSIDE EDGE

Now comes the real test of your control. Zigzag the pylon course and try skating on the backward outside edge starting five feet before the pylon. Turn all the way around the pylon and out toward the next pylon.

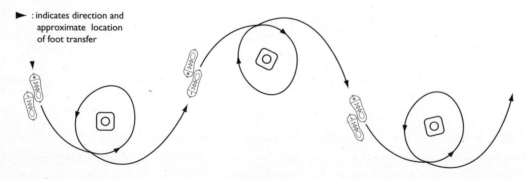

► : indicates direction and approximate location of foot transfer

BACKWARDS BOW - LEGGED WALKING (FROG WALK)

This drill will improve your hip turnout.

Walk backwards on your outside edges in a bow-legged stance. Make sure that your knee-bend is directly over the skating toe.

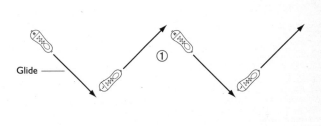

Glide

①

Variation: To improve your agility, use the same bow-legged stance but glide rather than walk (1). Before you change feet, cross behind the gliding foot then step down. This is tricky but can really improve your balance.

Variation: To further increase your turn-out, repeat the previous two drills while pulling a partner. Your partner should glide on two feet or provide you with some resistance by doing a snowplow skid (2).

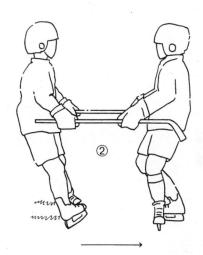

②

ONE - FOOT SKIING (SLALOM)

One-Foot Skiing utilizes both inside and outside edges. Just like in Two-Foot Skiing, the three track bases will be used: Wide, Basic and Narrow. Again, the key to sustaining movement is the knee-bend — use a slight up-down knee action, and a slight rise during the transfer from one curve to the next. Knee-bend is a must on the curve. To ensure the knee does all the work, carry the released foot low to the ice but behind the body. Perfecting this position is also important when you add shooting to this drill — the released leg will already be in position, and will be one less thing for you to adjust.

Use a track base as Wide as you can weave, taking the edge to its outer limits without losing control.

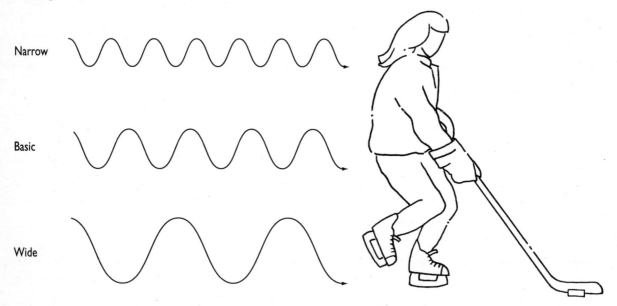

Narrow

Basic

Wide

Variation: Use the whole ice for a really wide track. Warm up using crossovers around the end of the ice. Then, on the board side of the face-off circle, push onto one foot, then glide in on the blue, out on the red, in on the blue, then out to the boards.

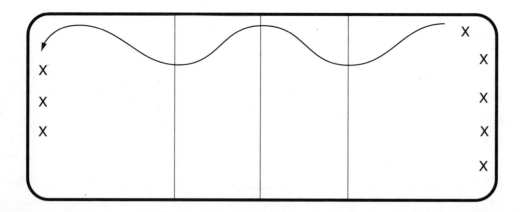

The Basic track is about two feet wide. Because this base is used for developing power, concentrate on bending the knee past the toe.

The Narrow track should be very tight. The Knee-bend is only deep enough to allow you to roll as fast as you can from one edge to the other.

Variation: Try shooting while performing this skill. If you are a right-handed shot, for your forehand shot skate in on the left foot, for your backhand shot skate in on the right foot. Start off at centre ice. Skate to the blue line, then go the rest of the way on one foot. Next, start in the corner. Skate to centre ice, then travel the rest of the way on one foot.

Note: For some players, Backward One-Foot Skiing is easier because your rear-end can swing a bit and help produce movement.

Variation: Advanced players should try this skill shooting backwards — it's real tricky. Start off at the red line. Skate backwards to the blue line, then travel the rest of the way on one foot. To shoot, twist slightly to the side but do not touch down or turn forward — that's too easy.

Advanced Variation: Skaters interested in agility training can start off with One-Foot Skiing forward, then turn backward on one foot without touching down. Continue backward, then turn forward again without touching down the released leg. Keep the released leg tucked in close to the body during the turn to avoid swinging. When turning from forward to backward, shift forward on the blade for the turn. When turning from backward to forward, shift slightly back on the blade.

Advanced Variation: For conditioning and balance training, add a stop. Push off as in the One-Foot Ski drill at the goal line, then stop on the blue line without touching down. Now start again still without touching down and stop on the red line; start again and stop on the blue line. Remember: don't touch down. Start once more at the blue line then finish at the goal line. Shake out the leg. The stops can be on the inside or outside edge. The key to the start is to shift slightly back from the ball of the foot then flick the blade out to start the weave — the Knee-bend must be past the toe! Try this drill both forward and backward.

I teach the players to pump their arms in the stride similar to a runner. Once I overheard a veteran from an opposing team tell a rookie to make sure he didn't come up behind Messier. He said "I don't know where he got it from, but he pumps his elbows really high." I related this to Mark and he just smiled and said, "Best thing you ever taught me, Aud."

•

The players on the Winter Hawks used to show off a bit when owner and General Manager Mr. Shaw and coach Ken Hodge came to watch. One year, a class had just got off the ice and I had put guards on my skates when Mr. Shaw and Coach Hodge came to ice level. Right away a fight broke out on the ice — John Kordic versus Brian Benning. Brian was younger and not nearly the size of John.

From centre ice I flew out toward them to break up the fight before Brian got creamed. I was well over the blue line before I realized how hard it was to move. I made the mistake of looking down — I still had my guards on! Then I wiped out — I should have never looked down. Shaw and Hodge were killing themselves laughing. I rolled over, took my guards off and winged them at them. Then I stood up and told John and Brian to break it up or else. John stopped immediately and glanced up where his father sat, knowing how he preferred John to play hockey.

I said, "Okay boys, apologize and shake hands."

John said, "Audrey, not in front of the guys."

"John," I demanded, "shake hands or I'll make you kiss him!"

John shook hands and apologized to Brian. I had to ban fighting at my camps … and quit wearing guards!

STRIDE

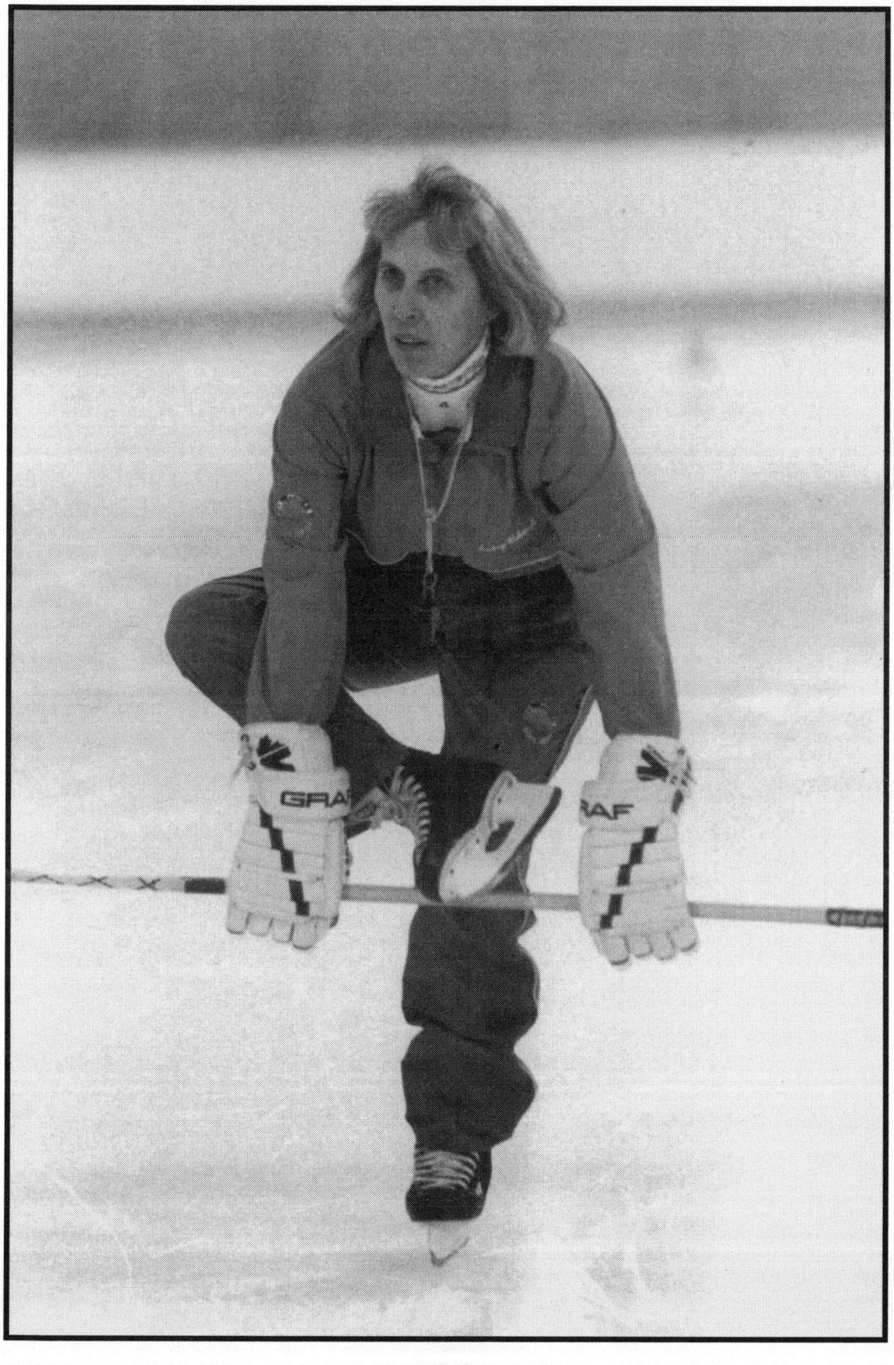
GRAF
RAF

C. J. RELKE

STRIDE

Body posture is the most important element in establishing an effective stride. The "Mark Messier" style emphasizes an upright upper body — when in full stride, you should notice a line through the body from the shoulder to hip to ankle.

Key Points to Remember: Keep your head up, stabilize the upper body using the abdominal muscles, keep your hips under the body, your skating knee past the toe, and the released leg thrust to full extension.

STRAIGHT LINE DRILL

The Straight Line Drill allows you to move slow enough to feel your position and to analyze the essential elements of a proper stride. Try to do this drill in slow motion so that you can correctly place your body in the required positions.

Draw a straight line across the width of the ice using the heel of your blade. As you perform this drill, you are going to trace this line. Prepare for takeoff: stand at the boards in a T-push-off position, with your back skate parallel to the boards (1). Make sure your back skate is balanced on either side of your line. For takeoff, the skating knee should bend at the same time as the pushing knee. After the push, the skating knee remains over the skating toe. The push is made with the ball of the foot. The initial push is down into the ice; finish the push by imagining the released leg pushing right through the boards. This helps to stretch the released leg to full extension (2). Once the knee is stretched to full extension, the leg remains straight with the released toe turned out at least 90° and the big toe pointing down to the ice. The stick held in front traces the line and is held with both hands (3).

The push on the stride should be at its maximum in the first six inches. The push is first down into the ice, then horizontal as the foot rotates 90° outward. The final thrust with the big toe ensures the full length of the muscles is used and guarantees full extension. Many instructors suggest pushing back on the stride, but I find that too many players tend to be lazy and bend the released leg at the knee, thus not using all of the muscles. By using the horizontal push, turnout is produced from the hip. A turned-out hip also encourages a horizontal return of the released toe. From the final thrust, the toe returns to touch the heel and then slides up the instep, ready for transfer.

Variation: Try this drill while stick-handling the puck about two inches on either side of the line.

Variation: To tell if your abdominals are stabilizing your upper body, try this: Put the knob of your stick on your belly button, extend your lower hand underneath the stick as a balancer, holding the stick out front, level with your belly button. Push off into the slow-motion stride and watch the balance of your stick. If the stick remains level, then your abdominals are stabilizing your upper body. If you collapse your abdominals, your hips will move back and your belly button will angle toward the ice. The dropped angle of the stick will indicate your posture.

Another way to check your upper body posture is to have someone watch the number on the back of your jersey. If they can see the top of your number, you have proper posture. If you are leaning forward, the number will be difficult to see.

Further variations on the Straight Line Drill:

TOE TAP

Toe drag indicates that the foot has switched to a vertical plane and is slower on the return because of friction with the ice. Switch back to a horizontal plane. To emphasize toe turnout on the released leg, tap the ball of your foot on the ice (1) while alternating steps.

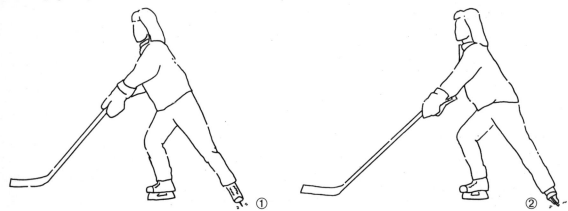

HEEL TAP

To feel the stretch of the inner leg muscles that should signal the full extension of the stride, try to tap your heel on the ice (2) while alternating steps.

TOE - HEEL - TOE TAP

Combine both taps together to improve your ankle awareness and agility.

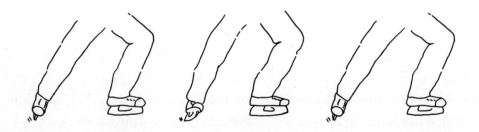

BOARD STRIDE

Use the boards to assist you in positioning the turnout of the released leg. Put the back blade against the boards (1) then slowly push out forward into a full stationary (on-the-spot) stride. Practice maintaining the knee-past-skating-toe position (2) while straightening the back leg at the same time.

HEEL DRAG

The Heel Drag is used to emphasize the required extension of the released leg.

Skate around the ice to gain speed, then push into a full stride, dragging the heel of the back leg.

CROSS - COUNTRY STRIDE

This skiing stride will stretch the groin and hamstring.

In a full stride, the groin should be used to help support the released leg. Try a cross-country ski stride up the ice: both blades remain on the ice. The trick is to maintain a deep knee-bend on the forward leg and still keep the heel of the back leg on the ice. Move the arms in opposition to the legs — left knee bent, right arm pumps forward.

HOURGLASS DRILL

The Hourglass Drill helps to build stride endurance. In a clockwise direction, the right stride (gliding on the right leg) is practiced, and a left stride is used when moving in a counter-clockwise direction. Start with crossovers or quick strides at the end of the rink. At the edge of the face-off circle, push into a full stride, glide to centre ice, and then hold until you reach the edge of the far face-off circle. Then wind up again.

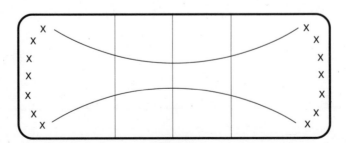

CROSSOVER STRIDE

Crossovers are covered in detail in the next chapter. Make sure you have your crossover technique down before practising the Crossover Stride. Skate around the ice zigzagging and alternating the Crossover Stride. Cross the right foot over and push on to a left stride. Then cross over the left foot and push on to a right stride. Keep your head facing forward.

Add visual balance to the drill by turning your head back on the stride, to check the full extension of the released leg. Make sure your head faces front on the crossover.

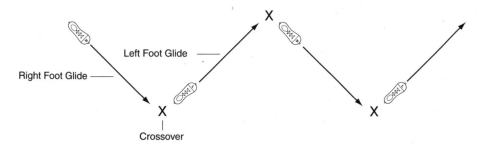

Variation: Under control? Then add a partner and a puck. Pass and receive the puck while holding the stride.

Variation: Practice timing, strength and coordination with your linemate by doing the Crossover Stride side-by-side using a horizontal stick for support.

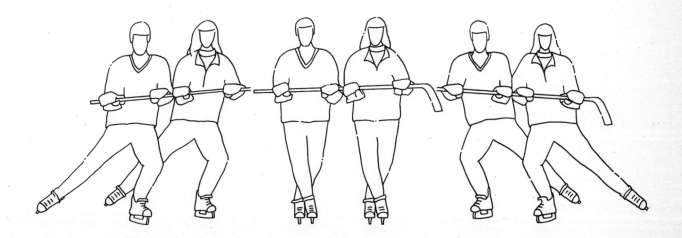

It is often a new experience for hockey players is to be placed or physically put in a position by a power skating instructor. In figure skating, because lessons are so short or positions so exact, an instructor just gets used to grabbing and putting whatever needs to be put in place.

When I first started working with Dave Semenko of the Edmonton Oilers I can remember trying to place his hip and encountering extra bulk on his sides. Without thinking, I said, "Hey, what have you got in here?" I whipped up his jersey and looked in the side of the pants. "Oh, just some extra padding for hits," I said, only to look up at a red-faced Dave. Poor Dave — that was the beginning of hours of endless drills I would come up with for him.

There was a huge size difference between Semenko and me — I lie and say I am 5'4" and get away with it because my posture makes me look bigger than I am. Many times I would do drills with Dave holding the stick and essentially pulling me along as I gave instructions. We would do this in a big circle, Dave on the outside of the stick working on crossovers, me on the inside going for the ride. However, it looked like I was supporting Dave and every time we did it a teammate would skate by and say, "Aud, will you hold me up next?" Dave would just smile and continue on.

CROSSOVERS

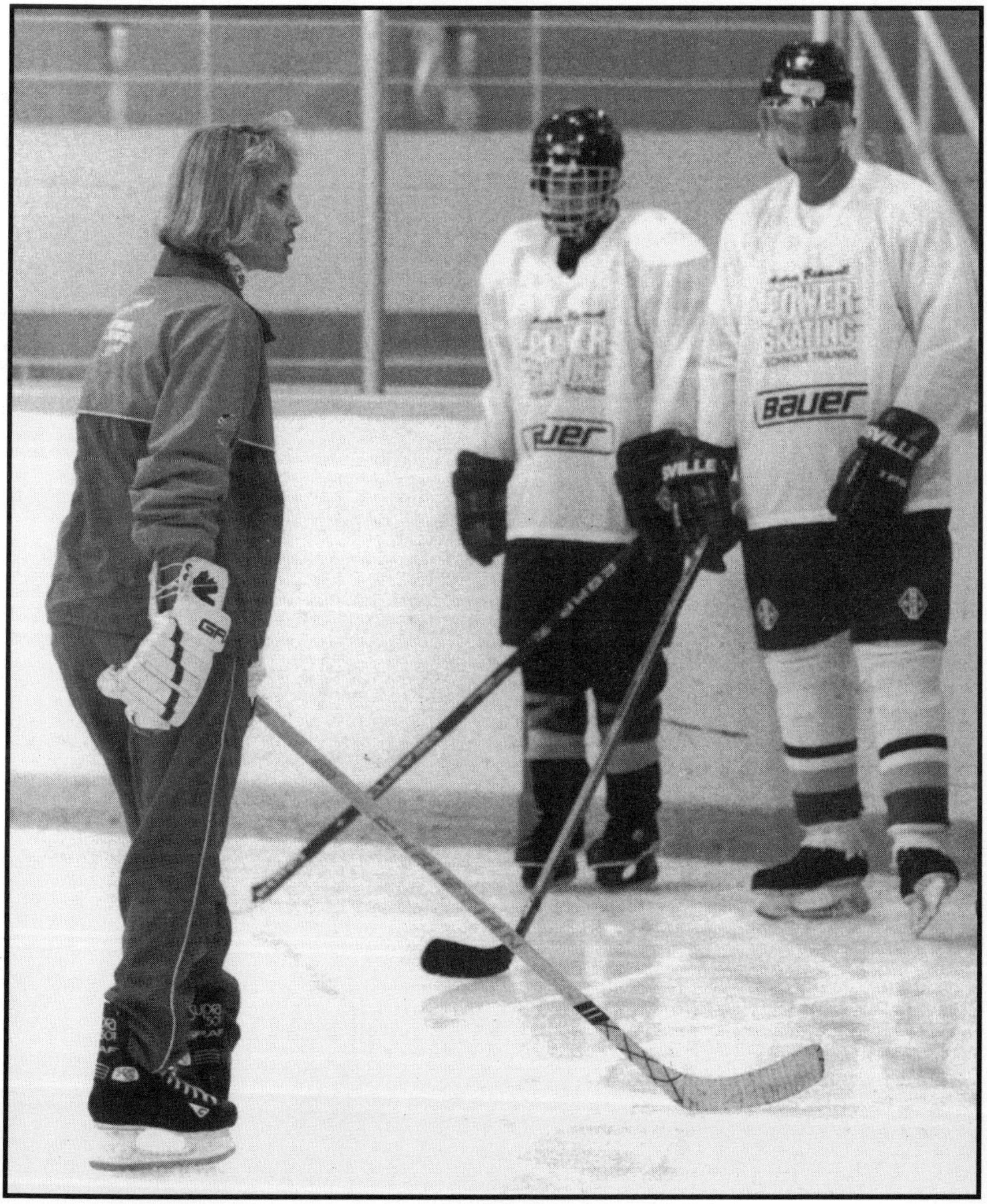
POWER SKATING
TECHNIQUE TRAINING
Bauer

C. J. RELKE

CROSSOVERS

Crossing one foot over the other is the most difficult task for the beginning skater. Practicing as many drills as possible, and crossing or tangling your feet up prior to learning the proper crossover method, increases confidence and agility. In some cases it makes the real crossover seem easier than the prerequisite drills. Many of these drills are designed to angle the hips diagonally and are difficult to perform if the hips dump back. Keep your shoulders level.

PRE - CROSSOVER SKILLS

Following are a number of lead up drills to prepare you for the proper positions and to help you become aware of the location of your heel and toe.

HEEL ON TOE - CAP GLIDE

It seems funny, but I've noticed that when the skates are on, a lot of players do not know where their toe and heel are. They know the width of the blade because of the edges, but not the length. The heel should cross over the laces when moving into the tuck position in the crossover, so it's important to have a sense of where your heel is.

Start off with this drill travelling in a straight line. Place the blade of the heel in the middle of the toe cap of the gliding skate. Make sure both toes point straight ahead. Hold your stick in a balance position.

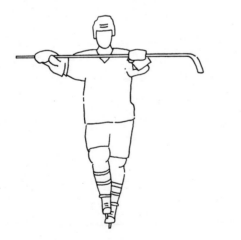

CROSSOVER TUCK

Drop the heel down beside the gliding foot, tucking the heel as far back as possible.

TUCK WEAVE

Stay in the tuck position but instead of travelling in a straight line, try weaving in a slalom pattern. Keep both knees slightly bent. Advanced skaters should add the puck to this drill.

CROSSOVER TOE TAP

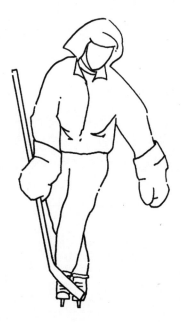

To make sure the tuck is as tight as possible, tap the toe of the back foot with the blade of the stick. Try to touch the little toes together. Alternate taps by crossing over, then tap, crossover the other foot, then tap, and so on. Again, this is a visual aid that helps a player be aware of foot placement rather than just going through the motions of a crossover.

CROSSOVER MARCH

March up the ice, lift the knee into the Knee Raise position (see Warm-Up section), then slide down into a Crossover Tuck. Alternate feet. The Crossover March is done slowly, tucking in each alternating crossover. Lifting the knee high makes sure the foot doesn't catch on the gliding foot. It also gives you time to set your posture before the tuck position. This drill is an important confidence-builder for the beginner.

CROSSOVER RUN

Try a sequence of alternating pigeon-toed crossovers. Stay down on your knees, crossing over in front with the toes as turned in as possible. Alternate the tempo from quick to slow. Notice the tracks are narrow when quick (2) and wide when slow (1).

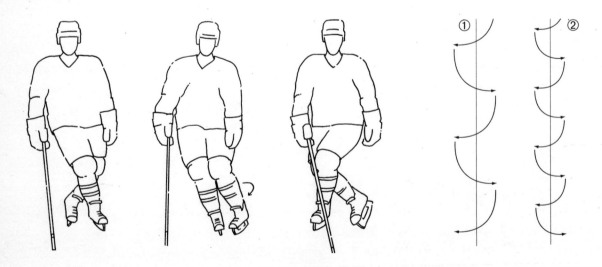

REXING

The Rexing movement will help to develop agility and increase foot awareness.

Rexing is an in-line skating term. It is a combination of In and Out and the Crossover Tuck. With both blades on the ice, push out then glide together, moving into the crossover tuck position. Try this with variations on your track:

For building power, use the Basic track and push hard on the Out motion and tuck tight when in the crossover tuck.

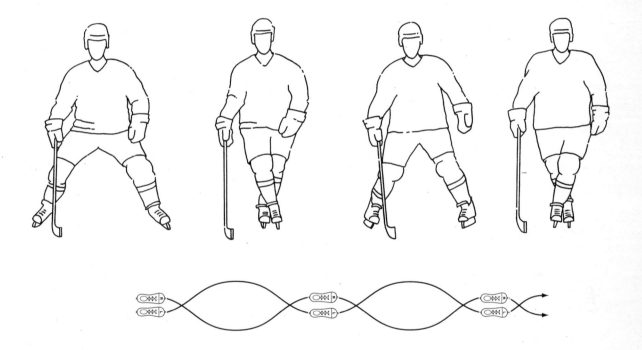

For agility, practice rexing using a Narrow base. Move the feet as fast as you can. The tuck is very quick.

For stretching, use the Wide base and instead of tucking tight, bend down and touch opposite hand to foot. The stretched leg should be pulled forward so that the big toes are on a horizontal line. The stretched leg should be straight and the knee on the bent leg should be over the toe. To stretch the back even more, reach the same hand to foot.

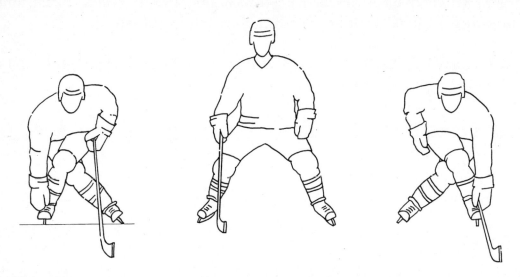

Variation: As the lower body does wide Rexing (1), twist the upper body around as far behind as possible. When the right foot crosses over in front (2), the upper body twist is to the left (3). Follow a slalom pattern — the push for motion occurs just before the curve using an outward scull. The crossover tuck-and-twist occurs on the curve.

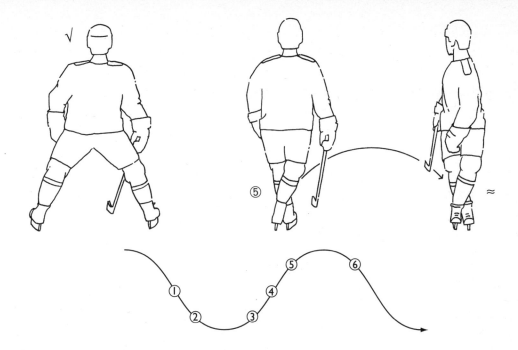

FLAT - FOOTED CROSSOVERS

In going through the full range of motion with both blades on the ice, the hips are forced to work under the body and angle properly for the most effective push.

Both blades remain on the ice throughout this drill. The outside foot pumps first to the side (1), then glides to the front and tucks in (2). The inside foot pumps under the body and outside the curve (3). The line of the body is diagonal from the hip to the baby toe.

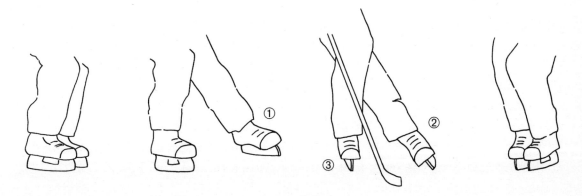

CROSSOVER PUMP

The Crossover Pump is designed to develop the push of the inside leg. You should remeaininthe crossover position for the entire drill.

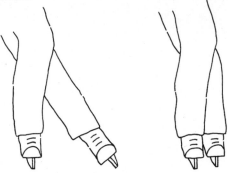

In the Crossover Tuck position, the tucked or outside foot on the circle is creating the push. The inside knee bends on every pump. This is a difficult skill at first because strategy, not strength, is the key. As in the Flat-footed Crossover, remember the diagonal line from the hip to the baby toe once the inside foot has crossed under the body to the tuck position.

For the Forward Crossover Pump, think of pumping horizontally (with the outside edge of the outside foot), then pulling forward to the tuck position. When in the tuck position, the outside of the skating boots touch together. For the Backward Crossover Pump, pump horizontally then draw the heel back to tuck beside the other heel. The pumping of the outside foot is the same action and pattern as in Sculling (In and Out), but it happens on the outside edge. This skill can be practiced on a straight line, on a face-off circle or on a very small circle using a stick to determine the perimeter.

CROSSOVERS

Crossovers are the most efficient way to skate on a curve and to keep the feet moving with power. In most cases, I refer to the pushing direction as horizontal rather than back. A lot of players lose their blade when pushing back, and by pushing horizontally you get a good grip on the edge.

Crossovers consist of two thrusts. These thrusts are only effective if you have neat footwork and position the pelvis on an angle for the carry-through of the second push. Try it out first in a stationary position. Stand beside the boards and use them for light support but do not lean on them. Stand with your feet together and bend the knees past the toes (1). Push the outside foot out horizontally to full extension (2).

From full extension, cross the foot over into a tight tuck. Remember the previous drills: draw the heel over the toe cap and tuck the heel as far back as possible (3). I use the tight tuck because it forces the next move to be on an angle and does not allow the hips to dump back. Now the back foot is the outside foot and it will push horizontally under the body to full extension (4).

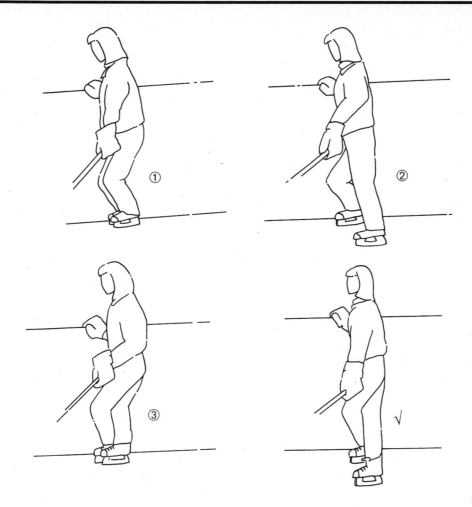

To further emphasize this position, have a partner pull your blade out horizontally as far as possible while you increase the knee-bend of the supporting leg.

If your rear-end is protruding, it is difficult to tilt the hips under the body, so it is important that your trunk not break at the waist.

STEP ONE - TWO - THREE - FOUR CROSSOVERS

The One-Two-Three-Four step breakdown for Crossovers is an easy progression which will highlight your strong and weak areas, making it easy to analyze and improve.

On a curve, move from Step One through to Step Four.

Step One is a horizontal push to the side to a full extension with the outside foot.

Step Two is the Heel on Toe-cap Glide. This is to remind you where your feet are and to ensure that you are actually crossing over.

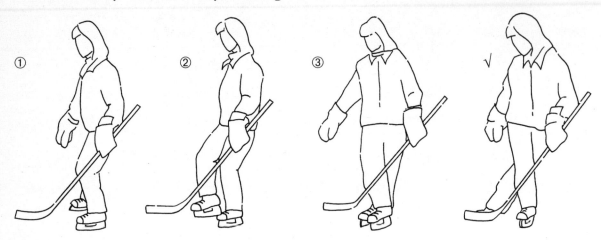

Step Three is the Crossover Tuck glide.

Step Four is the Crossover Tap. As your back foot releases from the tuck, cross it under the body and push it horizontally to the side. Once it is off the ice, slide it forward and tap it with your stick when it is as close to being in line with the other toe as possible.

FORWARD PUSH ONE CROSSOVER / PUSH TWO CROSSOVER

This exercise emphasizes the use of both legs to push. Most players use the outside leg to push on the circle, but neglect to let the inside leg cross under the body and also push.

Try regular Forward Crossovers, making sure to use Push One Crossover (the horizontal push of the outside foot (1)) and Push Two Cross*under* (the horizontal push of the inside foot (2)).

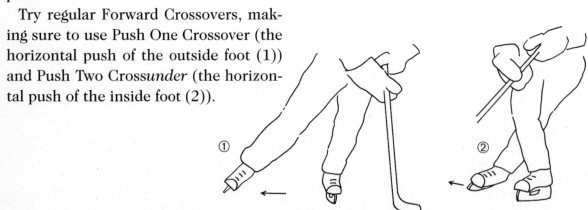

Note: Keep this in mind about the upper body — keep your sternum in the middle of the curve so that you can stick-handle on the circles. Keep your shoulders relatively square to your hips; this allows for stick-handling on the inside and outside of the curve. The figure-skating method of keeping the inside shoulder slightly higher does not apply to hockey or ringette because the inside hand may be the lower stick hand.

If you need extra support, have a partner glide on the inside and use the stick horizontally for support.

BACKWARD CROSSOVER

Most players keep their weight on the outside foot on the Backward Crossover, only momentarily changing that weight when crossing over. I prefer to keep the weight equally between the feet, as it is in the Basic Stance. As well, I make use of the adductor muscles for maximum power. To do this I use a Reach and Pull method. The inside leg on the curve reaches to full extension and grasps the ice with the inside edge. Then, using the adductor muscles, it starts pulling back to the body (1).

As the inside leg crosses under the body, the weight of the body is taken over by the outside foot (2) and the inside foot finishes with a full thrust to the outside of the circle (3).

If you need extra balance to practice Backward Crossovers, use a partner and your sticks. Hold one stick horizontally at hip height. Both players hold onto this stick with one player slightly inside the circle and gliding. The other player is working on crossovers. To emphasize the full reach, have the inside partner extend her stick inside the circle, just beyond the outside player's full leg extension. The outside player will try to step on the stick blade. This is like the carrot and the donkey trick — just as you go to step on the stick blade your partner moves it further away, making you reach that little extra but never actually allowing you to step on the stick.

BACKWARD CROSSOVER SHIFT

This next drill is especially for defense. If combines the Backward Crossover and Lateral Shift. Keep your head facing the opponent's direction and follow a zigzag pattern down the ice.

I call this the Paul Coffey Shift:

(1) Backward lateral shift to left side; pull with the right leg;

(2) Left leg crosses over;

(3) Backward Lateral Shift to right side; right leg should have full knee bend, left leg is fully extended;

(4) Left leg pulls, so right leg crosses over;

(5) Backward Lateral Shift to left side; left leg is in full knee-bend, and right leg is fully extended.

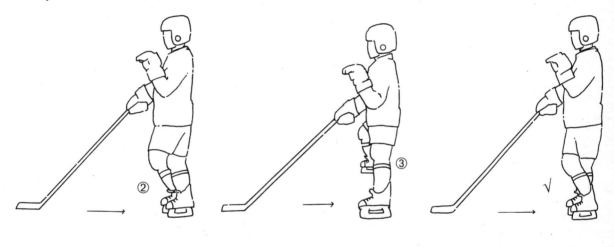

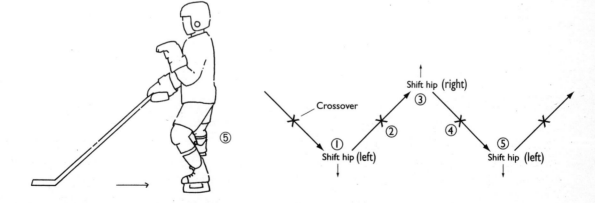

Variation: Rotate your head behind on the crossover (left leg crosses over), then face the opponent on the shift. This variation requires exceptional balance due to the head rotation.

PARTNER CROSSOVER SHIFT

This is a one-on-one simulation drill. Hold your sticks at hip level, facing a partner. Crossover and shift in the same direction at the same time. The defense player must react to the forward's movements and tempo.

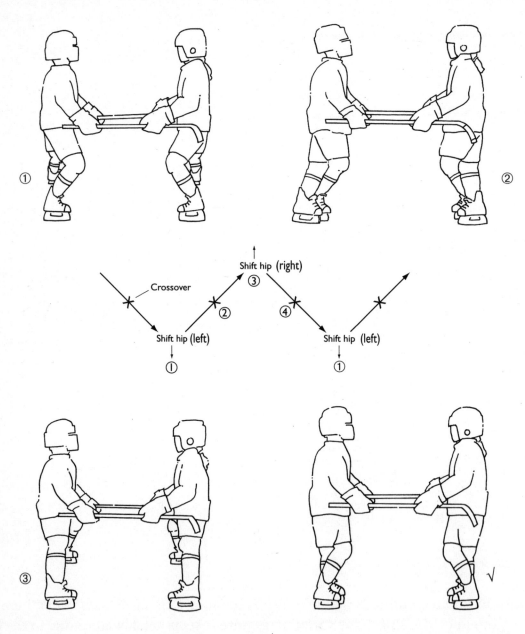

TURNS

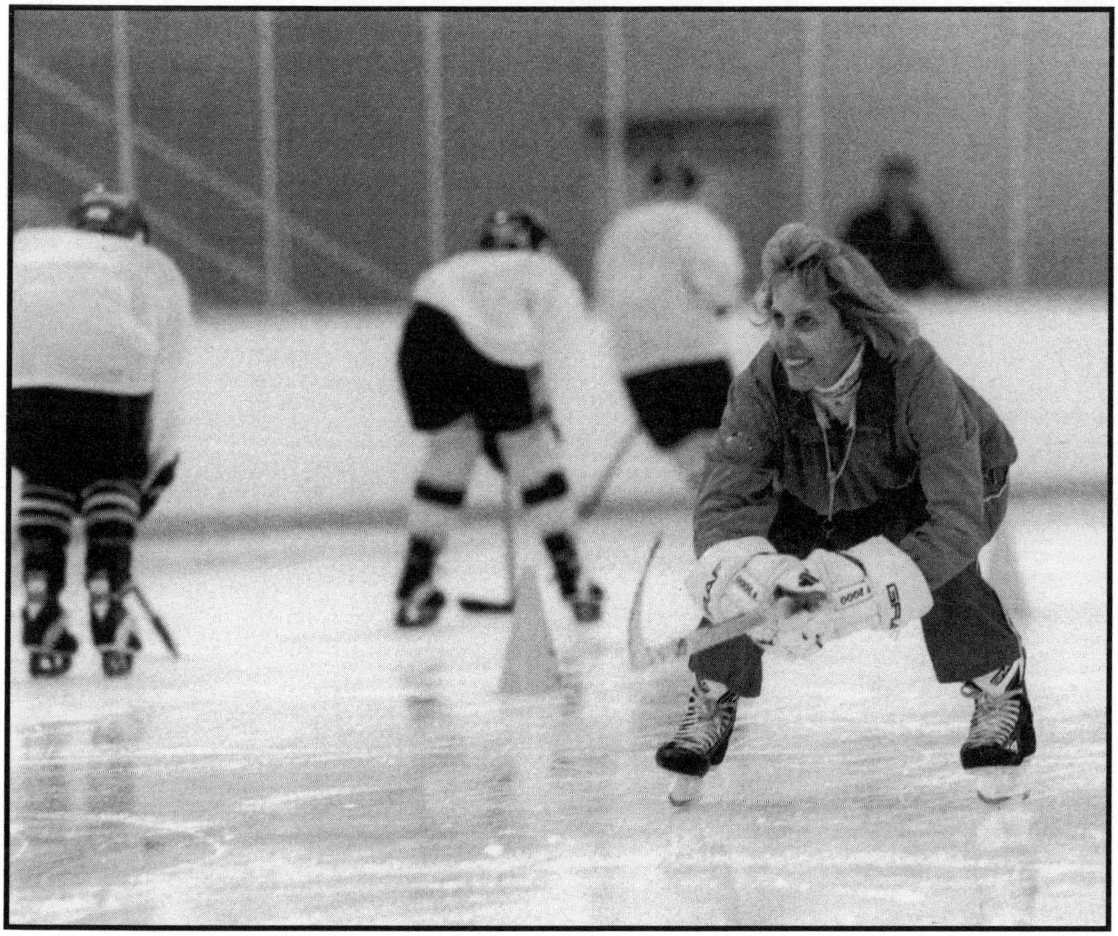

C. J. RELKE

TURNS

The Mohawk Turn is a figure-skating term that refers to a turn from forward-to-backward or backward-to-forward with a change of feet during the transfer. The name is believed to come from its resemblance to a movement performed in the war dance of the Mohawk nation. It is one of the basic elements of effective turn control on the ice. Before attempting a complete Mohawk Turn, you'll need to practice some basic control and agility skills.

PRE - MOHAWK TURNS

The Mohawk Turn is easier to execute if you have good turn-out from the hip. Here are a few drills to develop the turn-out required.

ONE - FOOT GLIDE

The One-Foot Glide is a good starter. Turn the released leg 180°, touching your toe (1), then your heel (2), to your skating toe while gliding in a straight line. Do this drill forwards and backwards.

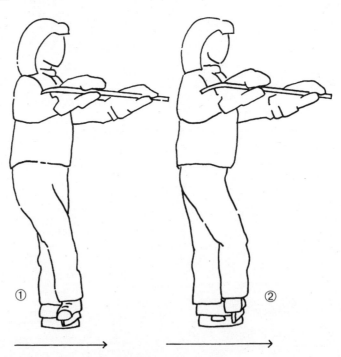

PIGEON - TOED WALK

To improve your hip rotation, walk forward pigeon-toed. Keep your toes as close together as possible and walk on the inside edges or flat of the blade (1).

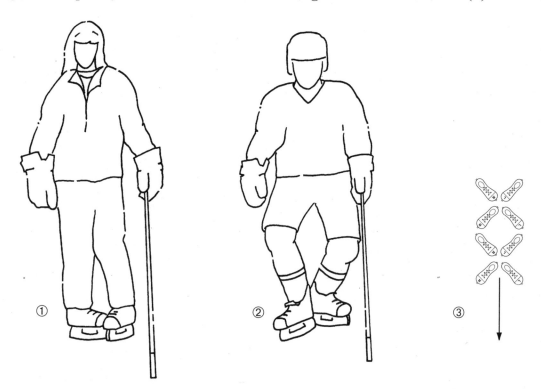

BOW - LEGGED WALK

To work on equal turnout on both sides of the body, walk in a bow-legged position. Keep your heels close together (2). Use the inside edges or flat of the blade when walking forwards. Use the outside edges or flat of the blade when walking backwards. The backward drill is a must for defense. It is important to all players because if hip turnout is inadequate, extra stress is placed on the knees.

PIGEON - TOED / BOW - LEGGED WALK

Work on your agility by alternating the Pigeon-Toed Walk with the Bow-Legged Walk, stepping from one to the other as fast as possible (3).

SIDEWAYS SHUFFLE

Again, use the Pigeon-Toed to the Bow-Legged Walk position, only this time try it shuffling to the side. To move sideways, put your weight on the lead foot and push slightly with the back foot. Turn your toes in and out as far as possible. Keep your weight on the ball of your foot.

SIDEWAYS TWIST

Another way to work your hips through the 180° rotation range is the Sideways Twist. Keep your upper body as stationary as possible. Point both your toes in one direction, then rotate your hips until your toes point in the opposite direction. At the same time, rock from the front to the back of your blades — like you're doing The Twist. Lift up on your toes, then rock back on your heels. You need excellent balance for this drill because you use the length of the blade as well as the edges.

BOARD SPREAD EAGLE

Use the boards for support to practice hip turnout. Face the boards and press your feet and knees in close to the boards with your toes turned out as far as possible (1). To really stretch the groin, bend your knees (2) and straighten again. If it hurts your knees with your hips fully turned out so that your heels touch the boards, then decrease the angle by moving your heels away from the boards.

INSIDE SPREAD EAGLE

You will be gliding when executing the Mohawk Turn, so to practice turnout while gliding try the Inside Spread Eagle. Glide with both blades on the ice (with the feet turned out as far as possible) facing the inside of a curve. Glide as far around the curve as you can hold, then stop and glide back to where you started.

MOHAWK TURN

A Mohawk Turn on the inside edges involves a change of feet while moving from forward to backward or backward to forward. The heels should come as close together as possible at the change-over point. I actually train the players to place heel to instep when practicing slowly — remember how much position will be lost as soon as you add speed to the move. The player's chest faces inside the curve travelled.

The 360° rotation Mohawk Turn is broken down into four steps using three phases. First the 1-2, then the 1-2-3, followed by the 1-2-3-4 Mohawk Turn.

In the beginning, try the Mohawk Turn on a curve, then practice it on a straight line. You will generally only use it on a curve but practice the straight line as well because it is more difficult and develops better turnout and overall body control.

1-2 MOHAWK TURN

Begin the 1-2 Mohawk Turn on the face-off circle. Face the inside of the circle, then start on the Inside Edge Forward Glide (1). Draw your heel in close to the instep, transfer your weight to that foot, and change to the Backward Inside Glide. During the transfer to the other foot, remain as bow-legged as possible (2).

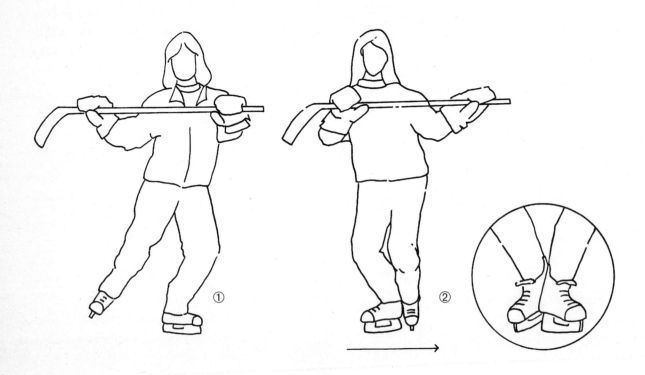

Now try the 1-2 Mohawk Turn on the straight line. Initially use the boards for support. Without your stick, use your hands to help direct you around the boards. Keep the shoulders level. Your hips must rotate easily to allow for a quick and easy transfer. Skidding is a common problem when first learning the Mohawk Turn. Lack of hip rotation causes the blade to catch and stop rather than glide. Try to twist your hips further around.

Variation: Get a partner and use your sticks for support. Have your partner pull on one stick as you change feet — this will help pull the hip around and assist in the transfer. Next carry the stick horizontally to control the upper body. Try to keep your shoulders level.

When transferring from one foot to the other, try to push off the ball of the foot and try to step onto the ball of the other foot. Earlier when executing the transfer, you may have noticed your feet were pretty close to a T-position. To make it easier to step onto the ball of the foot, point your big toe downward in the T-position and draw that instep into the heel. The knee turnout is at least 90°. Try to actually touch the heel and instep together. If you practice the touch when going slow, the feet will not move as far apart once you add speed. Your knees should turnout so that they are in line with and directly over your toes. Do not force them out further — let practice improve the turnout.

Next, carry your stick horizontally to control your upper body. Follow the goal, red and blue lines. Keep your shoulders level.

1-2-3 MOHAWK TURN

Now that you have the 1-2 Mohawk Turn mastered, move on to the 1-2-3 Mohawk Turn. Step three is the Defensive Sit position. Both feet are on the ice and the upper body is upright, square to the hips. Again, start on the face-off circle.

Move to the Straight Line Drill and practice equal turning ability by alternating turns on each side of the body. Remember — keep your head facing in the direction of your opponent.

As a defense player, it is to your advantage to rotate from your hips down. Keep your upper body as square to your opponent as possible. By doing this, you won't telegraph to which side you are going to break. When breaking open, use a V-push rather than a crossover. Using a crossover commits you to that side and a smart forward will watch for the inside foot to move into the crossed position and then will break for the other side, leaving you all tangled up.

Sometimes the shoulders can be too squared up. This blocking effect makes the backward-to-forward glide awkward and is the reason most defensemen crossover when breaking after the winger. With some extra hip rotation and a slight shoulder release, the squared-up position will not interfere with the turn. Use a partner to control your upper body while rotating from the hips down.

Posture is a common problem in the 1-2-3 Mohawk Turn. Check your sit position learned earlier in the defensive sit stance. Make sure your abdominal muscles are stabilizing your upper body.

1 - 2 - 3 - 4 MOHAWK TURNS

To complete the 360° turn, move on to the 1-2-3-4 Mohawk Turn. As you did before, begin on the face-off circle. Steps one and two are actually a forward-to-backward Mohawk Turn, and steps three and four are a backward-to-forward Mohawk Turn.

Step three is no longer the two-foot defensive sit position you used in the 1-2-3 Mohawk Turn. It is now a one-foot backward glide.

Use your stick to help direct your turn. Practice repeated turning so that when you have to do just one turn in a game, it will seem easy. If you get dizzy when turning, focus on the end of the rink after every turn.

Those are the four steps that make up the basic Mohawk Turn. Here are variations:

1-2 CROSSOVER MOHAWK TURN

The 1-2 Crossover Mohawk should be included in your agility training. Travelling in a straight line up the ice, a crossover fits in between steps 1 and 2 of the 1-2 Mohawk Turn. Alternate from side to side and try to keep your feet close together during the crossover step. The 1-2 Mohawk Crossover is done on inside edges.

BARREL ROLL

The Barrel Roll is a 1-2 Mohawk Turn on outside edge followed by a crossover to complete the 360° rotation. Using the face-off circle, rotate to the outside of the curve then crossover to the inside and step forward, ready for another turn in the same direction.

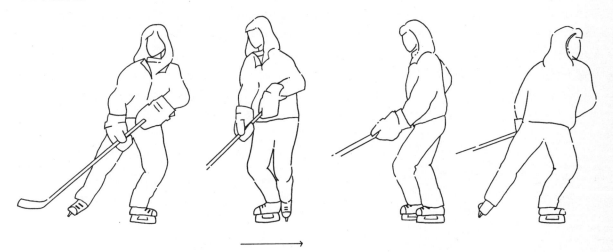

1-2-1 MOHAWK TURN

The 1-2-1 Mohawk Turn can be used when shooting. The glide of Step One is lengthened before and after Step Two. This forward-backward-forward transfer can be very effective in confusing the goalie. The shooter appears to be setting up a pass by drawing in the puck, but is really putting more body into the shot as he pushes back on to the forward glide.

THREE TURN

A Three Turn is a forward-to-backward or backward-to-forward change of direction using one foot. Your skates should leave a pattern on the ice resembling the numeral three. Push off on the face-off circle and try — on one foot — to turn from forwards to backwards and backwards to forward as many times as you can, always turning in the same direction. When you run out of steam, change feet but keep turning in the same direction. For example, travelling clockwise, start forward on the left inside edge (facing the inside of the circle), rotate the left shoulder forward into the circle and the right shoulder backward. This upper-body rotation will turn your body from forward to backward. Now you are on a backward outside edge facing outside the circle and have just completed a Left Forward Inside Three Turn (LFI-3 Turn).

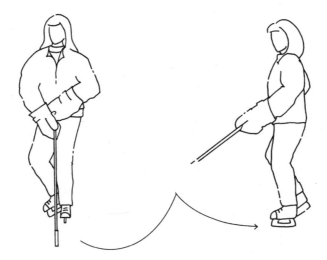

Advanced players will want to move forward on the front of the blade for a quick turn. To turn forward again, pull the left shoulder toward the right shoulder and pull the right shoulder back. This will return you to your starting edge — the left forward inside edge.

The second turn from backward to forward was a Left Backward Outside Three Turn (LBO-3 Turn) — advanced players will move backward on the blade for the turn.

Both turns were executed on the left foot without touching down at any point. By now you have run out of gas and are ready to change feet. Remember — the forward turn rotates into the circle and the backward turn rotates back into the circle — all rotation is clockwise. The next turn starts on the right outside forward edge. Use the same shoulder action — the left shoulder turns into the circle as the right shoulder pulls back. Now you are on a backward inside edge. You have just completed a Right Forward Outside Three Turn (RFO-3 Turn). Try the Right Backward Inside Three Turn. Rotate the upper body outside the circle — pull the left shoulder toward the right and pull the right shoulder back. You will find yourself on the right forward outside edge having just completed a Backward Inside Three Turn (RBI-3 Turn). Once you have control, try two sequences before changing feet: LFI-3 Turn, LBO-3 Turn, LFI-3 Turn, LBO-3 Turn. Change feet to RFO-3 Turn, RBI-3 Turn, RFO-3 Turn, RBI-3 Turn.

Got it?

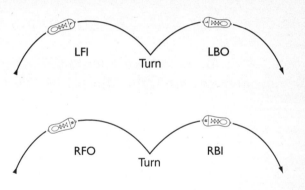

THREE-TURN SHIFT CROSSOVER

Earlier in the backward skating section, you did the Crossover Shift drill. Now add a Forward Outside Three-Turn. For example, do a counter-clockwise LFO-3 Turn (1), then shift to the right as far as possible (2), then crossover to the left (toward the boards) (3).

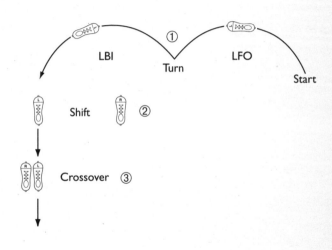

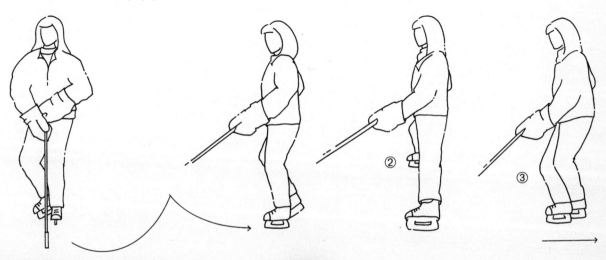

THREE-TURN SHIFT CROSSOVER / 1-2 CROSSOVER MOHAWK TURN

Make this footwork a little more difficult and see how good your transition and balance abilities are. To the Three-Turn Shift Crossover, add the 1-2 Crossover Mohawk Turn.

PIVOT TURN

The Pivot Turn will allow you to change direction quickly while gliding on two feet.

The Pivot Turn is also called the Tight Turn or the Glide Turn. Both blades remain on the ice with the toes pointing in the same direction, while performing a 360° gliding turn.

The inside knee on the curve is the control knee. The amount of knee-bend this knee has, along with the inward rotation of the shoulders, helps to determine the tightness of the turn. The outside leg is the navigator of the perimeter and the anticipator of the next step. I like to finish the pivot turn with a quick crossover or a quick push in the opposite direction. It is important that the outside leg does not get locked back, resulting in a slow turn. The more the outside shoulder rotates in on the curve, the tighter the turn.

Where the weight should be on this turn is a controversial subject. In practice, most players put weight on the outside foot, back on the heel and cut deep into the ice. In a game, however, the weight tends to be forward because you are cutting after a player or carrying the puck. I tend to put my weight on the inside knee when cutting tight or teaching, and on the outside leg when lazy.

Note: The shoulder action on the backward pivot is to the outside of the circle. It is easy to break at the waist and stick out your rear-end. Remember — when travelling backward, you should lead with the rear-end and keep it tucked under.

At the end of one camp, Winter Hawks team captain Brent Peterson came up to me and asked me to take off my gloves. My only experience with gloves coming off, especially with this team which sported players like Larry Playfair, Dale Yakiwchuk, Paul Mulvey and Doug Lecuyer, was for a fight. I did not know what to expect and tried to keep my gloves on; they pulled them off and presented me with a beautiful bouquet of roses.

•

A couple of years ago, Brent Peterson's son Brad attended my school. After class one day his mother came out of the dressing room laughing. Tami said that I would have to hire her son as my Public Relations director. He had been very seriously telling the player next to him that his dad would never have played in the NHL without Audrey's training!

•

The Portland Winter Hawks were a very popular team, particularly in the eyes of young ladies. After the Memorial Cup in Portland, the walls in the banquet room were covered with paper. Fans wrote notes to each player. As a huge line-up of fans filed around the room, three young female fans were in front of me. They kept borrowing my pen to write suggestions to each player. I followed right behind scratching out their suggestions and writing to each player, "You have a lot of work to do this summer, now practice this, this, this and this!"

STOPS

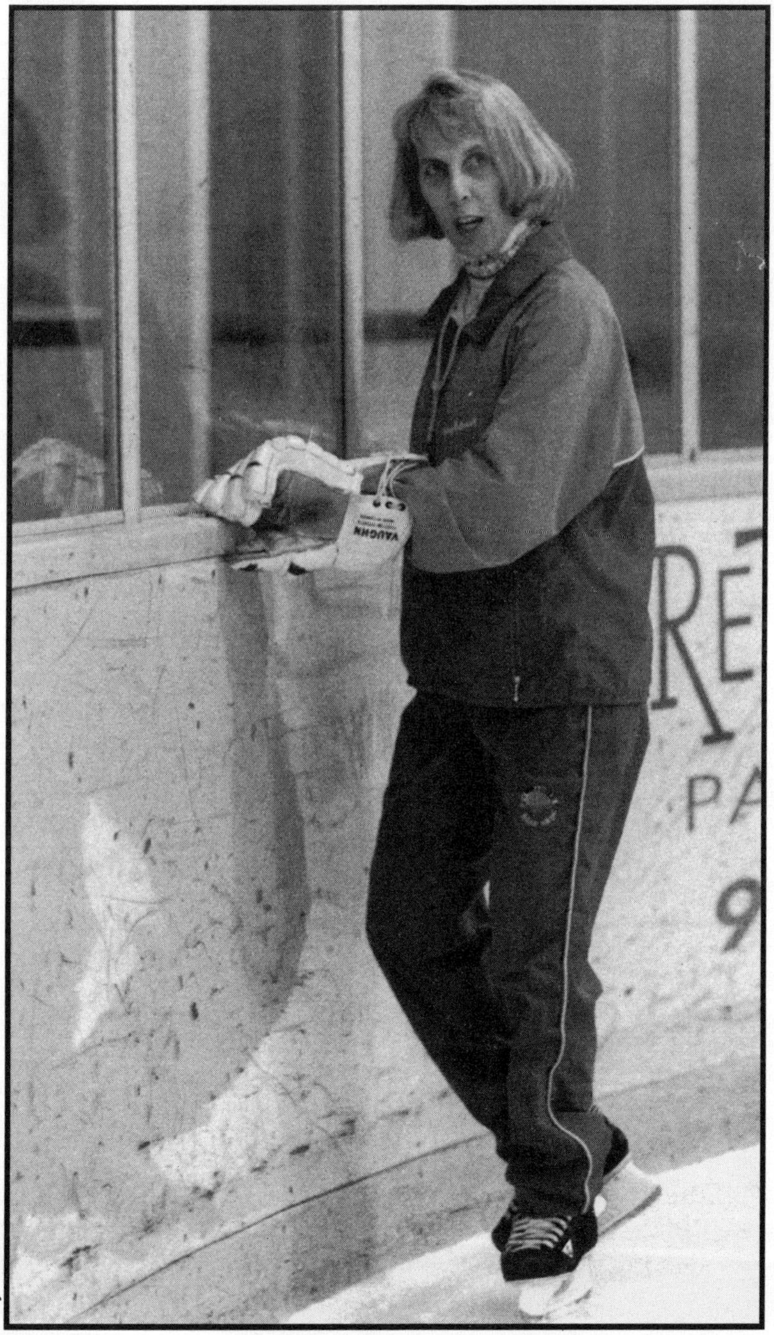

VAUGHN

C. J. RELKE

STOPS

I prefer teaching a combination of a Side Stop and Snowplow Stop to beginners. I do not like to teach the snowplow initially because too many youngsters lock their knees together, stiffen and end up wiping their nose off the ice. I teach the Two-Foot skiing-to-side stop method, but most beginners actually start out using a half-snowplow in the ski stance. This works well for beginners — I would rather have them remain standing and confident.

HALF - SNOWPLOW STOP

The Half-Snowplow Stop is used to stop with one foot while gliding on the other. It is used frequently by defensemen who must stop and back up quickly. Initially, glide up the ice on one foot. With the other foot, lightly skid on the inside edge (1) gradually increasing pressure until coming to a stop.

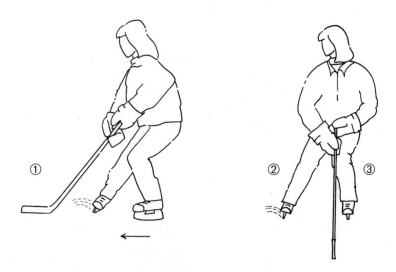

SIDE STOP

To learn the Side Stop, start out two-foot skiing, then turn to the side and push the lead foot into the ice using the ball of the foot on the inside edge (2). Some players use the outside edge of the following foot to stop as well. I use that foot for balance and keep the knee bent (3), ready for the next action.

ONE-FOOT SIDE STOP

The One-Foot Side Stop is the same as the Side Stop, except that you balance and stop on the lead foot. For example, if you are stopping counter clockwise, the body turns left, and you stop using the right foot on the right inside edge (1). Tuck the left foot in to the Step-Touch position (with your toe tucked in to the heel).

Try the One-Foot Side Stop using the inside (1) and outside edges (2). The key position is the basic body stance and knee-past-toe position.

BACKWARD SNOWPLOW STOP

The Backward Snowplow Stop requires excellent hip turnout. Turn your feet out as far as possible and push into the ice with the balls of your feet, using the inside edges.

SNOWPLOW STOP

I use the Snowplow Stop for conditioning. With a partner, tuck your sticks in at waist level. Keep your stick tucked in towards your ribs for support, and so that you cannot swing. One partner travels forward and the other travels backward while doing In and Outs at the same time and pace. On the whistle, both stop using snowplow stops. Without picking your feet up, change direction and continue with In and Outs until the next whistle, and so on. Remember to use deep knee-bends on the stops, and to pay attention to your upper body posture. Breaking forward at the waist on the stop only makes the change of direction and start up more difficult.

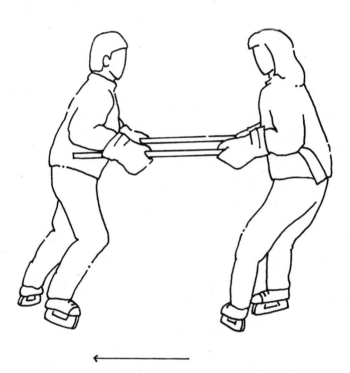

←————————

AGILITY

C. J. RELKE

AGILITY

Now that you know the basic skills — Stance, Stride, Edges, Turns and Stops — it is essential that you maintain and develop them while also building on new skill areas. Agility is an important attribute of any good skater.

JUMPING

Jumping is a good agility drill as well as a balance and muscle-builder. Remember to take off and land with good knee-bend, with your head up and your stick carried in front. Keep your feet together.

SKI JUMPS

Start skating down the ice skiing on two feet. Once you have momentum, start hopping left to right, slalom style.

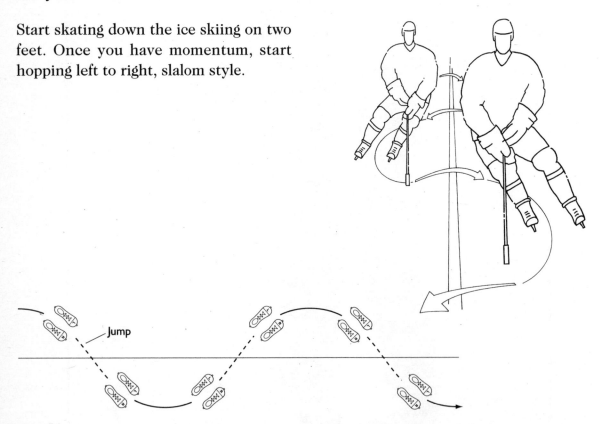

TWO - FOOT FORWARD - TO - FORWARD JUMP

Set up a series of jumps along the blue lines. Place the points of two pylons toward each other, on their sides. Skate from the goal line, take off from two feet and land on two feet. To condition your thigh muscles, stay in a full squat between jumps.

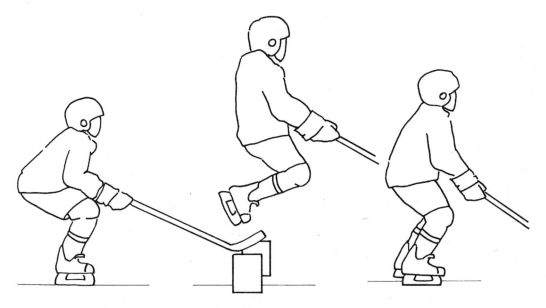

ONE - FOOT FORWARD - TO - FORWARD JUMP

Try a one-foot forward takeoff to a one-foot forward landing, using the same foot. For conditioning, bend down between jumps and touch your toe cap with your stick.

TWO - FOOT FORWARD JUMP - TO - SIDE STOP

Take off forward on two feet. Rotate a quarter turn in the air, and land in a side stop. For example, if you started off facing East, when you land you should be facing South. If this is too difficult for beginners, try a Two-Foot Forward-to-Forward Jump and then ski into the side stop.

ONE - FOOT FORWARD JUMP - TO - SIDE STOP

If you are an advanced skater, try the One-Foot Forward Jump to the One-Foot Side Stop. Do the side stop on the inside edge because this tends to be the more stable stop. It is easier to line up the knee over the toe. When first attempting this drill, make sure your weight is right over the knee for landing, and hop rather than leap.

TWO - FOOT FORWARD - TO - BACKWARD JUMP

Go back to the Two-Foot Jump, but this time take off forward and land backwards on two feet. Keep your head up and remember your rear-end has to rotate with you.

TWO - FOOT FORWARD JUMP TO BACKWARD SNOWPLOW STOP

Again, try the Two-Foot Forward to Backward Jump, only this time land in a Backward Snowplow Stop.

FOOTWORK

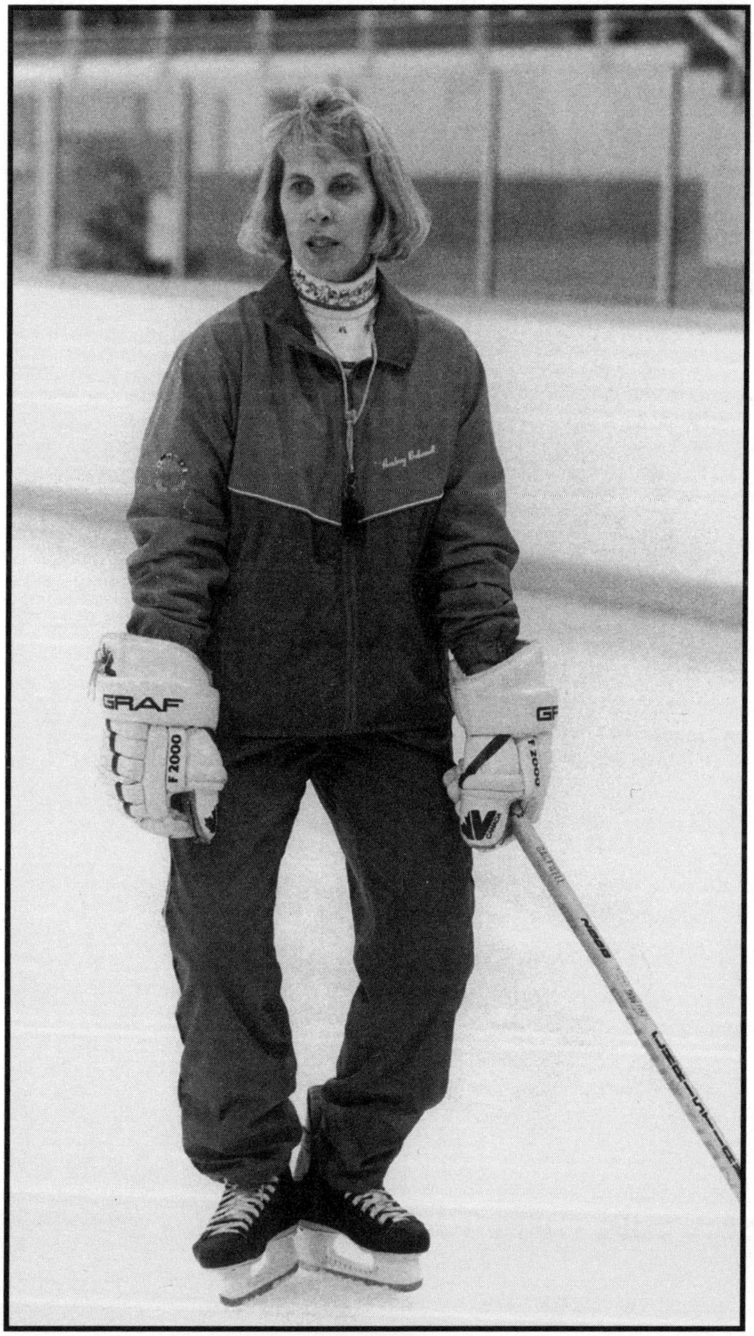
GRAF
F 2000
F 2000

C. J. RELKE

FOOTWORK

There is more to the blade than just the edges — it is important that a skater know the length of the blade. The following drills are designed to get you up on your toes, the ball of your foot and your heel.

TIPPY TOES

This drill requires the knees to remain bent and past the toes. You are going to slide using the front part of the blade right by the plastic. Both blades stay on the ice and you scurry up the ice as fast as possible.

HEEL SLIDE

Rock back as far as you can on the heels. Pull both sets of toes toward your shins and slide up the ice on your heels.

TIPPY TOES - HEEL SLIDE - TIPPY TOES

Alternate from toes to heels to toes all the way up the ice.

JAZZ STEP

This is an excellent agility drill because it requires edge control, balance and speed. This is a step drill — you must centre your weight and place your edges so that you do not glide or skid. Imagine a straight line up the ice — you are going to move up that line. Place your left foot on the line, then cross the right foot over in front (1). Make sure the right foot is tucked in on the line. Put your weight on the right foot, then draw the left foot out and extend it as far to the left side as possible without shifting any weight to it (2). The left foot will touch down on the ball of the foot on the inside edge for a split second. As it does, the right foot steps up and back down (3) ready for the left leg to return and crossover in front (4). Then the right leg extends to the side, and so on. This is called a step-ball-change sequence; as you do it, repeat to yourself: crossover-touch-tap. It can also be done with the cross behind the support foot (5).

Note: In all the footwork and agility drills, you should keep your stick in hand, usually extended in front.

POLKA STEP

To get the weight on the ball of the foot, try a Polka Step. Step-hop-hop is the easiest: from a stationary position, take a side step to the left. As you place the right foot by the left, raise the left (hop). Lower the left foot again and raise the right (hop), stepping wide back to the right. Continue the sequence with a brisk rhythm. Start off Polka-ing on the spot, and eventually try moving in a straight line up the ice. To further improve your balance, turn your body around as you are practicing.

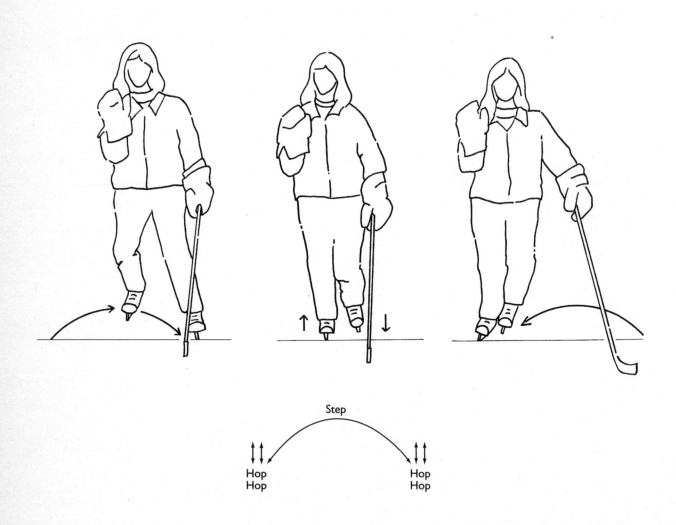

TWO - FOOT SPIN

Without a stick, stand stationary on two feet. Extend your arms (1), swing them (2), then pull them in tight (3). Keep your elbows up at shoulder height. You will find yourself spinning on two feet. Extend your arms to make yourself stop (4). Remember to keep your eyes open.

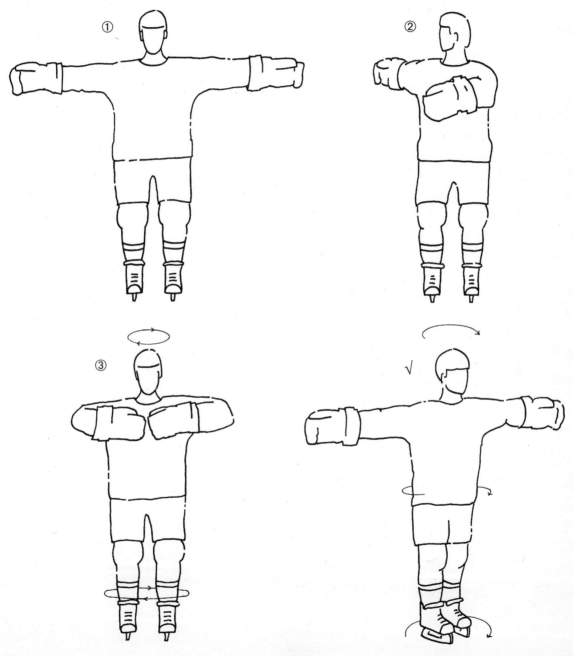

TWO - KNEE SPINNERAMA

Spinnerama is a fun drill, but it also teaches balance and visual focussing while turning. As you may have guessed, most of my training is based on overload. Drills are practiced from one extreme position (wide to narrow, stretch to agility) to the opposite end of the spectrum. If you repeat a skill thirty-five times in practice, then it will be easy and natural to do it in a game situation. This is especially true of turning and learning to visually focus while turning.

The Spinnerama is one of my favourite drills. It requires clean ice. Start at the end boards. Skate hard to the blue line then gently drop down on both knees. Pull your arms in as you drop, creating a spinning force, and spin as far as you can. Your upper body should remain erect — keep your elbows up for stability. If you are doing this with other players, always wait until the player is over the blue line before you start. If you run out of steam or fall, get out of the way quickly. If you have trouble focusing after turning, stare at a specific object like a pylon when you come to a stop.

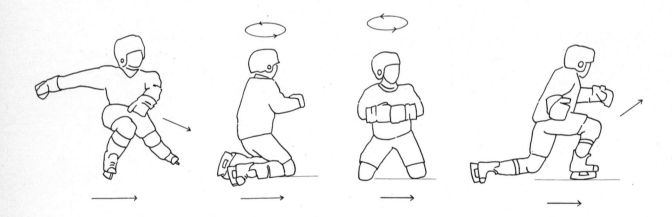

ONE - KNEE SPINNERAMA

The One-Knee Spinnerama requires more control and concentration. At the blue line, drop down on one knee, do one rotation, then hop up, skate and drop down on the other knee at the next blue line. Do one rotation then get up again. Add the puck to the turn. Pass it ahead or tuck it in.

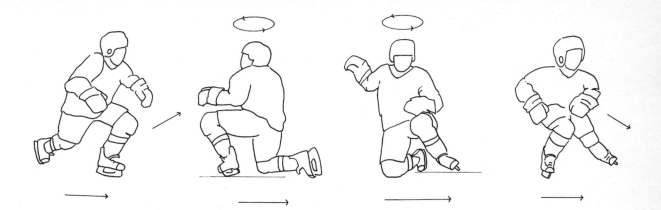

MOONWALK

This is an agility drill requiring use of the entire length of the blade. This drill is excellent for increasing knee-bend. Do a backwards Moonwalk: start skating backwards, then slide on the flats of the blades. Point the toe of one blade down as it slides back. Point it down at a 90° angle so that you can grab the front of the blade by the plastic and slide through the length of the blade while pulling the other gliding blade in under the body with the same motion, as if cycling on a bicycle. Keep the flat of the blade on the ice for the glide.

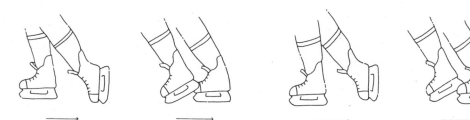

I lay no claim to fame to teaching Wayne Gretzky how to skate. When he first came to the Oilers, Glen Sather sent me out to put him through a workout and assess his level. Wayne followed me through some drills and I thought, "This is more like it!" Wayne skated at the level I expected from the pros, and I had not yet realized the mental level Wayne was at. Later, while working for the Oilers, I would be doing a drill with another player and Wayne would skate over, follow me for a while and then take off to other things.

One day I came out to practice and must have looked a little worse for wear. Wayne skated over and said, "Okay, today you follow me!" I was tired that day and so after a couple of steps, I hauled Wayne down with my stick. Unfortunately, Al Hamilton's son, Steve was on the ice before practice and thought this was a great game. He jumped on top of Wayne to wrestle. I made myself scarce.

•

People in the media often ask me who I think is the best skater in the NHL. I always answer that there are players who are outstanding in certain aspects but that there was not really a best skater. Fortunately for me, many of the best individual skaters played for the Edmonton Oilers while I was working with them, and I was able to watch them endlessly for several years. I think that Paul Coffey was the best backward skater; Mark Messier had the best stride; Glenn Anderson had the most extreme balance range and Wayne Gretzky had the best agility and endurance. What more could you ask for in one team?

CONCLUSION

There is never just one way to do to anything. In using this book, take only what will help *your* game. Keep in mind that, when learning new techniques, you should be critical of the skill but not of yourself. If you say, "I can't do this," then chances are you will not be able to. Acknowledge when you make a mistake and then get on with doing whatever it is you are going to do to make it better next time. Be open to new ideas and start each session with, "I will …"

Design a practice plan. The amount of time that you can spend practicing strictly skating skills will depend mainly on ice availability. You may have to do it just before or just after your hockey or ringette practice. Try to spend at least fifteen minutes focusing on skating skills; if you have to, split the time into warm-up and cool-down time. Of course, I would like to see you practice every day. But just like all other exercise advice: at least three times a week.

To get to the point of performing a skill without thinking, you may have to practice the progressional drills as often as the actual skill. An additional benefit of practicing the progressional skill is that it will transfer technique to other skills. For example, the Inside Spread-Eagle — or Frog, as I often call it — is used in a hockey game to maintain movement on a curve. The Frog requires exceptional hip turnout just like the turnout required for the Mohawk Turn, so two skills are improved.

The number of skating skills you practice in one session is up to you. I suggest that you sit down with a monthly calendar and schedule three practices a week. Each practice will focus on a different skill. For example, Monday — stride; Wednesday — backward skating; Friday — forward crossovers; Monday — tight turns, and so on.

Mark off each practice you actually complete. Maintenance of your skating skills during the season is very important and is best accomplished by repetitive practice following a consistent schedule. Have you noticed in your personal life that when things get frantic, work piles up and stress takes over, the first thing to go is your exercise schedule? A similar thing happens in hockey: the team may not be playing very well and the coach starts focusing on systems or strategy. Or the season just seems so hectic that the basics are forgotten. Having good intentions to practice but never *actually* practicing the skills usually explains why eventually a player finds that she is not moving as easily or as efficiently. No matter what — keep up your technique training throughout the season!

The players often discuss problems with the assistant coach or with me when I come in to work with a team. I was working with the New York Rangers farm team in Denver and the assistant head coach was Doug Soertart. I was in the coach's room one morning when a couple of players stuck their heads in looking for Doug.

It turned out that one of the players had been in a car accident the night before and when his teammates went to help him out, they realized that he was living in his car. They found plates and silverware. The team was still staying in the hotel and no one had noticed that, to save money, this player was saving his per diem by staying in his car. The team immediately housed him. Later in the year at a fan-club dinner each player spoke about another player and then about himself and his ambitions. This player announced he was going to buy a van for next season.

REFLECTIONS...

I thought this book would never be published.

I wrote the initial version of this book over twenty years ago. I tried many, many times to have it published in Canada — I can lay claim to having been rejected by the best in the business. The answer was always the same — unless it included sex, politics or scandal, the industry was not interested in how-to sports books. Hockey books were only published every seven years, and it was also blatantly pointed out to me that I was female. As if I didn't know.

Dave Elston, who often sits with me at Calgary Flames games, had had his books published by Polestar. Dave suggested that I call his publisher. I thank Michelle for her immediate enthusiasm and encouragement.

Michelle asked what stage the manuscript was at. I told her it was at the *dejected* stage, meaning that I had just been turned down for funding on my how-to video, and had pounded out my frustration on my computer by rewriting my book. I guess, then, that one rejection helped to create an acceptance. Michelle thought it looked pretty good, and agreed to publish it.

Ten years ago, I finished a Master's Degree in Interactive Laserdisc Technology. I tried to produce a laser disc on power skating, but, of course, ran into another series of funding rejections. Education was the leader in laserdisc technology, but because of funding cuts, the focus was shifted to the military and health, who were concentrating on simulation.

Eventually I re-focused, and produced my own power skating video, *Get The Edge*. Today the CD-ROM and interactive market has reopened in education; my next goal is to rewrite both book and video into this new technology.

I find it interesting that, after twenty years and all the technological advances that I have witnessed, I'm here with a book — a book that you can open when and where you want to, flip to any page you need, look at for as long as you like — no power required, no buttons to push, no screens to burn out. And the technology of hockey has not changed, either — I'll always be telling players to *skate from the hips down, and play hockey from the hips up*.

My work has finally been published. Thanks to everyone involved.

NOTES

NOTES

Polestar publishes some of North America's best-selling sports titles. These books are available in your local bookstore, or directly from Polestar. Send a cheque for the retail price of the book, plus shipping and handling costs: $5.00 for shipping the first book in your order, and $2.00 for each subsequent book. American customers may pay in U.S. funds.

Allstar Hockey Activity Book
Noah Ross & Julian Ross • $6.95 Can / $5.95 US
Hockey history, Soviet hockey cards, and hours of hands-on fun for young hockey fans.

Behind The Mask: The Ian Young Goaltending Method, Book One
Ian Young & Christopher Gudgeon • $18.95 Can / $14.95 US
Drills, practice techniques, equipment considerations and more are part of this unique goaltending guide.

Beyond The Mask: The Ian Young Goaltending Method, Book Two
Ian Young & Christopher Gudgeon • $18.95 Can / $14.95 US
Book Two of this effective goaltending series focuses on intermediate goalies and their coaches.

Celebrating Excellence: Canadian Women Athletes
Wendy Long • $29.95 Can / $24.95 US
This collection of biographical essays and photos showcases more than 200 athletes who have achieved excellence in their sport.

Country On Ice
Doug Beardsley • $9.95 Can / $8.95 US
The story of Canada's compelling attraction to the game of hockey.

Elston Shorthanded
Dave Elston • $9.95 Can / $7.95 US
Elston's sharp-edged wit and unerring shtick-handling pokes fun at your favourite teams, players, coaches and managers.

Elston: Back To The Drawing Board
Dave Elston • $9.95 Can / $7.95 US
Sports-cartoonist Elston's comic view of the world of hockey.

Elston's Hat Trick
Dave Elston • $9.95 Can / $7.95 US
The third in this best-selling cartoonist's collection of irreverent, hilarious hockey cartoons.

Hockey's Young Superstars
Eric Dwyer • $9.95 Can / $8.95 US
Profiles and action photos of Bure, Jagr, Lindros, Mogilny, Sakic, Modano and others.

Long Shot: Steve Nash's Journey to the NBA
Jeff Rud • $18.95 Can / $16.95 US
A compelling chronicle of an elite athlete's journey through high school sport, national team play, NCAA, and—finally—the NBA.

Lords of the Rink
Ian Young & Terry Walker • $18.95 Can / $14.95 US
Discover the inner workings of the game's most intriguing player in this final book in the Ian Young goaltending trilogy.

Rocking The Pond: The First Season of the Mighty Ducks of Anaheim
Dean Chadwin • $10.95 Can / $8.95 US
The chronicle of the creation of one of the most successful expansion teams in NHL history.

Taking The Ice: The Mighty Ducks of Anaheim
Dean Chadwin • $5.95 Can / $3.95 US
A young fans guide to the Ducks, including interviews, stats, photos and stories from the early days.

Thru the Smoky End Boards: Canadian Poetry About Sport and Games
Kevin Brooks and Sean Brooks, eds. • $16.95 Can / $14.95 US
The glory of sport is celebrated in this anthology of poems from more than seventy poets.

Order from:
Polestar Book Publishers
1011 Commercial Drive, Second Floor, Vancouver, British Columbia, Canada, V5L 3X1   (604) 251-9718 / Fax (604) 251-9738